Seeking My Daughter Faith

Parables From The Forgotten

"But by the grace of God I am what I am"
(1 Corinthians 15:10, NAB)

Debra Marie DeLash

ISBN 978-1-64416-056-5 (paperback)
ISBN 978-1-64416-080-0 (hardcover)
ISBN 978-1-64416-057-2 (digital)

Christian Faith Publishing, Inc.
832 Park Avenue
Meadville, PA 16335
www.christianfaithpublishing.com

This is primarily a work of fiction. The characters, names, incidents, organizations, and dialogue in this novel are either the products of the author's imagination, author's own experiences or are used fictitiously.

Printed in the United States of America

Prologue

My stomach hurts every morning when my father is loaded. Breakfast turns to burning pain as time in the woodshed looms large. His words haunt me still, "Only wimps cry."

As a quiet teenage boy, I stuffed my anger. Sitting in that church pew every Sunday next to mother I wondered, *why didn't God protect us?*

Though over sixty-five years have passed, I can still hear father's booming voice. "Only wimps cry."

Before leaving for school this day, I open the woodshed door to see father's tall, muscular body leaning against the doorjamb, slowly snapping that blasted razor strap against his thigh. He is shirtless, with deeply tanned arms and pale torso. His memory makes me want to upchuck.

My young self walks slowly toward the smiling man in the doorway. I am forced to squeeze through father's sweating body. The windowless room darkens as the door quietly closes. There is complete silence, except grunting before each slapping sound of leather against my skin.

We all have pain, with so many forms of suffering seen in our world. Some folks must carry the sins of others from an early age. Others meet evil much later in life. My own father's pain created a poison in the lives of those he touched; his pain dripped and dripped into my young spirit. Yet as a grown man, for years I held this dream of a do-over with my earthly father, a primal need to somehow have that happy ending. Most people would not understand such a desire. I hardly did myself.

I married at nineteen, found a job, and ran away from my most treasured relationship, with eldest daughter, Faith. You see, the feelings I stuffed inside as a child had silently grown until one day, I hopped in the car and drove away from everyone I loved. Trying to escape the past, afraid of watching my teenager, Faith, suffer from her emerging mental illness, I took off in my car and kept driving. And though three thousand miles away and a whole new life, my soul could never find rest on any other path but the one I left behind.

My name is John Goodwill. This is my story of finding faith, hope, and love which is God's gifts for all His creation. I have discovered that what broke my heart the most, screaming so loudly that eventually every cell in my body could hear, directed me toward my soul's true calling. This story is my efforts to heal my soul before I die.

Next time you see an RV going down the road, take a pause and think of me, reflect on all of us. Sometimes God sends help wrapped in the most unexpected packages. As long as we have breath, there is a second chance for a do-over with the ones we love, and with ourselves. This will be no ordinary journey.

Acknowledgments

1 am not sure how often this section of the book is skipped over; please bear with me while I give proper attention and gratitude to those whose inspiration and guidance helped make this book possible.

To give honor first and utmost to God for without his spirit, mercy, forgiveness, and love, I would not be writing to you today.

To my mentor on the original draft of this story, Sharon Levine. Back in 2012, the idea of father's RV trip came into my heart, and I could not let it go. As I was dealing with a back injury, confined to a chair for eight months, awaiting surgery, Sharon gave selflessly of her time and talent. She would spend hours reading and editing my e-mails containing story ideas, then once the first draft was completed, listened as I read it over the phone every Saturday morning for five weeks. She laughed, cried, encouraged, and was a wonderful writing teacher to this raw pupil. Thank you, Sharon, for help with the powerful description of several of the characters and narratives for this story. In 2016, I resurrected the manuscript, rewriting several drafts, and now it is coming to fruition. I cherish your guidance, the gifts of your writing, artwork, and past support for Loving1withmentalillness. May God keep you always in His loving care.

To those who are living with a mental illness or love someone with mental illness, I dedicate this story to you. As I see this published, many societal challenges and obstacles remain surrounding mental illness: access to treatment, limited financial resources, long waiting times to see fewer psychiatrists, growing homeless populations, a shortage of crisis and locked unit psychiatric beds, and overflow of people with serious mental illness into prisons and jails. My hope is that through this story, the reader will take a closer look at the reality for those afflicted and their loved ones.

On a more personal note, to my esteemed friend and father of my eldest daughter, Mike. Mike lost his life at thirty-three years old, dying from suicide. He is one of many tragic faces of those lost far too early by this dreadful brain disease. His memory is echoed into the words of several powerful scenes I have included within this story.

To my parents who passed away over twenty years ago. I miss you both every day. My mother, who gave freely of her love, faith, and support, and my dad, the most humorous, kind-hearted soul who always told me to believe in myself, as he believed in me.

And finally, thank you to my husband Joseph. He has stood by my side for thirty-three years so far, through good times and bad, better or worse, and in sickness and in health. His love is my guiding light.

Chapter 1

There but for the Grace of God, go I.

—Unknown

A Father's Journey: John Goodwill
The Year 2013
Santa Barbara Harbor, California

State Street is a long, roughly three-mile artery which runs from the eastern border of Santa Barbara westbound and leads directly to the harbor. It is a thoroughfare for residents and tourists alike, a visual smorgasbord of our diverse human experience. With my daughter Hope busy with Skype phone calls, I decided to round up my grandson, Frank, and invite him for a drive to visit the waterfront.

Parking was easy to find on a Monday morning, and Frank had no problem maneuvering his 2009 Kia Rio into the harbor's normally busy lot. I am miffed at the new process of putting a bank card into those parking contraptions, punching through the glare on the keyboard to answer questions, and finally, if you get lucky, out will pop your ticket. Then, one must walk back to the car to place it properly on the dashboard. They ought to pay *me* for the time it takes to do this. Just because they can do something doesn't mean they should. I long for simpler days.

"Come on, Grandpa, let's walk the pier." Frank flashes an award-winning smile, and I imagine he has no lack of girls interested in a date. I wonder why Frank is not in class today. My own father valued education, and this is a trait passed down generations. I'm dying to say something, but I make it a point not to ask too many questions. Time spent with him is precious.

There are a few men fishing off the side of the pier, alongside small groups of sightseers. Frank and I take our time. I have always loved the water and remember forty-five years ago when I drove out to California from my hometown of Massachusetts.

I had been driving all night and pulled into an inviting hotel on the Hwy 101 stretch between Santa Barbara and Ventura in 1968, the Rincon Beach Hotel. I can never forget watching the first sunrise as it came over the coast range mountains to light up the waves, the shimmer so intense it was almost blinding. That morning I fell in love with the Pacific Ocean.

Frank interrupts my trip down memory lane.

"Now that is an interesting sight." I don't think Frank has ever seen the homeless flea market. He sounds annoyed.

Directly below the pier, we see a succession of handmade stations created to attract the attention of passersby. Every station has a different theme, and in the middle of each is a dish set up for visitors to drop coins. Designed by people who are homeless, this is a makeshift fundraiser. Theirs is an attempt to survive that shows amazing creativity. I'm not at all sure I could manage that in their place.

Possessing a reliably mild year-round climate, Santa Barbara attracts a large number of the homeless. Walking down State Street, you see fancy stores and expensive restaurants. Right next to these displays of wealth, men and women are found with no place to sleep but in doorways and alleys. They tote their earthly belongings on their backs. Side by side the homeless survive a minimal existence.

Set up on the beach there is one station which promises your wish will come true if your coin lands in the dish and doesn't bounce out. Another offers a cheap, plastic doll for the lucky participant who lands ten quarters into his dish. Frank laughs at the gutsy soul who asks you to rate your skills as a lover by dropping the coin in dishes marked as cold, fish-like lover all the way up to red hot mama. As my grandson only carries plastic currency, I retrieve a pocket full of coins, and we sample the various setups. Turns out I am a better lover than my grandson! This may be the high point of my week.

And then I saw him.

The homeless man appears to be pushing fifty years old, though he could have been younger. Living on the streets ages a person. He is talking to two men dressed in expensive suits, business owners perhaps. One of them holds those complicated cameras that ensure your heart's desire, at the very least. The camera is aimed at a beautiful sand figure of Jesus, built by this ragged, unshaven artist.

"Yep, I sculpt this 'Praying Jesus' every day. I have been making sand designs for thirty years now."

"Do you mind if I take a picture of this?" One of the businessmen asks the artist.

His eyes dance and nod consent.

I move in a little closer.

"Sir, what is your name?" I hold out my hand in a gesture of friendship and introduce myself.

"My name is John Goodwill," I tell him.

His hand feels calloused, his face scarred from years of sun exposure and life on the streets. Yet his spirit is still alive, shining out of his eyes.

"Bob." He says, "Just Bob."

The two businessmen finish snapping their picture and leave without a word or donation.

"How did you learn to sculpt like this?" I am more than a little impressed.

The man seems vibrant while he entertains my questions. Frank rolls his eyes and walks off.

The two of us sit on the sand, and I listen to stories of art, beach survival, and life. On previous visits to the harbor, I had noticed this curious artist before, yet this is the first time I slow down to have a conversation. I realize how much I have missed. I thank him for his time and company and tell him I would stop by again.

Deciding to give my grandson his space, I wander over to visit the Apple Man. The Apple Man is well known in Santa Barbara as he walks up and down State Street carrying a big box of Granny Smith apples. Rumor is he has a relative in Santa Paula who monthly brings him fruit from his orchards. He buys his own food with the money earned selling this produce on the streets.

As I walk toward the harbor through the white sand, which from the pier is about a quarter of a mile, I notice with annoyance that I have to stop and catch my breath more than once. I hate this growing old stuff.

There is a scruffy fellow already there as I approach the Apple Man. His appearance is typical of the homeless: a child's sled with rolled-up sleeping bag, plastic jugs with water, and a growing collection of recycling bottles. There is an old bottle jack included among his loot. Perhaps he is expecting a flat tire.

"How much do you charge for twelve apples?" he asks the Apple Man.

The Apple Man hardly lets him finish. "No, no. Here, for you, they are no charge." He pushes them into the man's hands.

The homeless man reaches into his baggy, worn denim pants, holds up a battered gray leather belt, and pulls out a brown wallet. The wallet has to be thirty years old, perhaps, the same age as the man who carries it.

"I want to pay. What do you charge?"

I glance sideways into the billfold, which contains roughly five one-dollar bills.

"Please sir, I want you to accept the apples as a gift," the Apple Man tells him.

The young man aims his steely blue eyes squarely at the Apple Man. He slowly retrieves three of the worn bills, counts them out, and places them on the edge of the fruit box.

"You have to eat as well, my friend. Take this, with my thanks."

I thought about paying for the apples myself, then recognize the mixture of self-preservation and pride, and keep quiet. Humility, honor, and believing that what is seen on the outside isn't the only thing worth embracing remain vital commodities the homeless possess.

I head back toward the pier. My stomach growls as a reminder it is time to go home. I imagine Hope has lunch ready. Perhaps pork chops with buttermilk gravy, an old man can wish, can't he? I hear someone scream, "Hey man, that quarter is mine!"

There is a growing clamor, and with each passing second, sand begins flying in all directions. Soon, several of the homeless men from the individual fundraising stations are in the mix, taking sides. Apparently, one of the tourists has dropped a coin from the pier, trying to strike the dish of the plastic doll station. Instead, the station with the fortune teller finds the coin on his blanket. The various blankets which hold these makeshift stations are placed so near, I imagine this is a frequent diversion from the boredom.

"Finders keepers, losers weepers," one of the men begins to yell.

There is no such notion in their lives that for them to fight over one quarter is absurd. But then, it isn't really about the quarter.

The man with the plastic doll station is barely five feet four inches. He runs up and decks the other man nearly a foot above him in height. They begin to throw punches at each other and are soon rolling around on the sand, down the row of merchants, who are cheering the combatants on. Occasionally, some of the other vendors jump in to help their favorite.

I couldn't help noticing that this gathering group of warriors is rolling dangerously close to my new friend, Bob, and his sand art, "Praying Jesus."

I see Frank sitting toward the end of the pier, and I yell my loudest.

"Frank! Get down here *now*."

A number of cell phones and Blackberry devices on the pier are suddenly in use, no doubt to summon police.

The homeless herd is now colliding into the belly of the Praying Jesus. With little respect, the sand which had so carefully been packed to create the sculpture is suddenly pulverized.

"You destroyed my Praying Jesus!"

The artist disintegrates into a diatribe of fear, anger, and paranoia. As I hear the sirens in the distance, his rants lose touch with reality, picking up memories of every indignity in his memory banks. The most significant reason for the light in his eyes and pride in his talent has been mindlessly destroyed.

Frank returns at the moment the police choose to subdue this innocent artist with the power of the almighty Taser. He collapses down onto the sand in helpless pain next to the shambles that his beautiful labor of love has become.

"Not safe around those homeless. This is why I avoid the downtown area," Frank whispers and takes my arm to move away.

"He is a gifted artist, Frank. The police punished the wrong man."

This homeless artist is like the shattered pieces of glass from a broken goblet. With each day, each moment, will he reflect and magnify light that touches him, or will he lose hope and block the light, to reflect only darkness?

As we walk away, I send up a small prayer that his rare gifted spirit will survive this sad day.

Chapter 2

I have never forgiven myself for my cowardice.
—Debra Marie DeLash

John Goodwill
Hope's Home
Santa Barbara, California

My youngest daughter, Hope, lives in the east foothills of Santa Barbara, not in the mega-money Montecito area but in an older neighborhood made up of an illogical mixture of vintage twenties, thirties, and forties architecture. Each one tells a story of where the original builder came from. There are gray and white Cape Cods, southern colonials with big white columns, and galleries, which are called wrap-around porches in California. There are Italian villas and small adobe homes, with terra-cotta roofs, which were made of native clay in this part of the world.

One of the old adobes is my daughter's house. She's a writer of self-help books, and one about designing Web sites hit it big and paid for the old house and extensive repairs a few years ago. She has a small separate building with lots of windows looking out on her garden where she does her writing. There is no bathroom or phone out there.

When Hope first bought the property, she explained, "I would never take a break if there were a bathroom out here. Necessity makes me get up and walk through the garden to the main house, at which time I remember to eat something. As for no phone, that's obvious. I have never liked the damned things, and I let the phone in the house pick up messages. Those who understand my writing accept my wishes."

After my grandson dropped me off at the house, he drove off on important business at his position at the Goleta News. Going in search of Hope, I want to share the impact of the beach scene. If I find the courage, I will drop my personal bombshell.

The house is silent except for the Siamese cat, who always assumes that any human being crossing the threshold is there to feed him. I am hesitant to interrupt my daughter in her writing cottage, but the time is long overdue that I tell her the truth about my past, present, and dubious future, if she will allow the interruption, that is.

I knock politely on the double Dutch front door. But she doesn't hear the knock, as the stereo is blasting the Beach Boys "Surfin' USA" at full decibels. I have to let go of courtesy and really bang loudly. The music is turned down, and she appears in the window with a frown on her forty-two-year-old face.

"I need to talk when you have the time," I say, trying to maintain calm and look harmless.

"Oh well, I've stopped now anyway. Let's go out to the garden. I have seeded wood violets under the oak tree I need to check on."

I walk behind her in silence, trying to find the right words. How do you drop a double bomb on your own child?

"I hardly know how to begin. You know I have trouble sharing private things, even with you, dear."

"I'm listening, Dad, just dump it out. It won't be as bad once you have said it. Didn't you use to say something like that when I was little and hit a baseball through the neighbor's kitchen window?"

"It's not fair to throw my words back, you know," I smile, glad for a few seconds of light before a dark subject.

"It's just that many years ago, when I was nineteen, I had more hormones than brains. My high school girlfriend and I got pregnant and had to get married. It was long before I knew your mother." I am becoming out of breath, which is not unusual these days.

Hope stops poking at emerging seedlings with the oak twig, turns around slowly, and sits down on a cast iron chair under the tree.

Her expression is more numbness than anything else as she just sits there, staring. I stare back, waiting for some kind of reaction.

"I think we had better go inside and have a drink. I'm sure there is more to your story than that brief paragraph."

I follow her into the kitchen, where the cat's "feed me" litany begins. She ignores him, goes to a bar of carved Mexican wood, and pours two glasses of vodka and orange juice. She leads me into the living room of bright colors and woven fabrics, where she sits down.

"So what happened to your other family, and why you are telling me now?" She always gets right to the point, no beating around the bush. I could have used a little dilly-dallying.

"We had a daughter, and we were happy for quite a few years. I was in construction, and buildings were going up almost overnight. More work than we had men to do it."

"What happened?"

"I'm getting there, be patient."

She gets up, refreshes her drink, and returns to the sofa.

"When Faith reached puberty, she began to change. She would be fine one moment and then fly into wild and destructive tantrums at the drop of a hat. Sometimes I could hear her talking to herself alone in a room, and suddenly, she would enter into a rage. She was kicked out of school and sent to therapy. We all went to family counseling. Nothing was working. I wondered if it was my fault. My wife and I got little sleep, as we never knew where she was or what she was up to."

"What happened?" she repeats.

"I was supposed to show up for yet another counseling session and lost direction, physically and emotionally. Instead of meeting them at the psychiatric hospital, I took a wrong turn and headed out of town westbound toward the ocean. I just kept going. I don't have a good excuse, except I had no preparation for what was happening. I hoped things would sort themselves out if I just went away for a while."

"Then what?"

"I checked into a beach motel, mailed a letter to my wife and daughter with a return phone number, saying I needed to stay away for a short time. I called a week later. When the phone calls began, they were strained, angry, and unproductive. It was always about blame, giving blame or taking it all on myself. I could not see any way out of the suffering, which I had compounded by running away. I have never forgiven myself for my cowardice."

"How are they now?"

I am tearing at my cuticles yet continue, "We divorced in a few months, sold the house. She and our daughter moved into an apartment near the clinic where they were treating what they now call bipolar disease. I got a construction job here along the coast and never went back. I sent money every month, but I just could not face what I did. When I would work up the nerve to call, my wife would cry, and my daughter would hang up. That was the script until I finally said there was no more point to it. I told them how to reach me if they wanted to, but they never called."

"Was your daughter's treatment successful at any point? Lord, it feels weird to refer to someone else as your daughter."

"The last I heard she was in and out of a community college, sometimes taking medication, most times not."

"Where did all this take place, for God's sake?" Anger is creeping into Hope's expression. She has gone from numb, to shock, to curiosity, to impatience, to anger, in just half an hour.

"In Massachusetts."

"Massachusetts! What the hell were you doing in Massachusetts?"

"My father's family lived in a prerevolutionary house in Boston."

"So I assume everyone in the family knew, about your first family, and just lied to my face whenever necessary? Holy shit, Dad! How could you not mention this? All those years when you preached about character, integrity, telling the truth no matter what! How could you live with your own hypocrisy?"

Then, as an afterthought, she turns from her third trip to the bar and says, "I don't even know who the hell you are anymore." She takes two more steps and turns again to say, "I wondered about my name and if there existed a Faith or Charity anywhere."

"I'm your father and love you as I always have. And, no, there has never been anyone named Charity in the family."

"Oh, that's a *big* help. Why are you telling me this today?"

Oh dear Lord, I thought, *we need to get to the second half of the bomb.*

"I need to find my other daughter and try to make amends."

"Ha! Fat chance of that, I suspect. I repeat, 'why now?' And I wonder if you would have abandoned me too if I had turned out defective."

I begin to deny this when she interrupts with, "No, I'm sorry. That is unfair."

I continue on quickly before I lose my nerve.

"You have noticed that my health is sliding downhill. I just can't escape from this any longer. If I could have spared you this pain in the process, I would have. But I have spent forty-five years being chicken-hearted. So my mistakes spill onto you, and I am very sorry."

"You're making speeches, Dad. You know how I hate that. I love you, but at the moment, I need some time alone, because I don't much like you. I'm going back out and try to concentrate on my work, maybe figure out how I feel about all this. Heat up the enchiladas in the oven, will you? Just the two of—" As she charges out the door into the garden, the last words are lost.

I walk into the kitchen to pour my drink down the sink. This is hard for an alcoholic to do. I can almost hear the silent scream, "*Noooo*, don't throw it out!" Being a member of Alcoholics Anonymous is another secret I have kept. For now, though, I need to catch my breath and quiet this fast-beating heart. I have never really told anyone how serious my health issues are. That is something to look forward to!

Chapter 3

Hope sustains us throughout life. But in the end, it is Faith that leads us home.

—Debra Marie DeLash

John Goodwill
Hope's Kitchen
Santa Barbara, California

A s the morning sun fights its way through rough linen curtains, I enjoy a brief moment of ignorance, forgetting what happened the night before. But not for long.

Hope never came in for dinner. I finally ate overcooked enchiladas and watched some TV in the guest room, falling asleep with David Letterman. He had some forgettable teen rock starlet, whom I thought to be devoid of any real talent.

I shower, change my slept-in clothes, and head down to the kitchen, where I can smell the coffee.

My grandson is saying to his mother at the stove, "You promised last year that if I moved home you would stop asking where I had been all night. Remember, Mom?" Frank's tieless shirt and khaki's look slept in and probably have been. His Topsiders are worn without sox, a style his mother really hates. I hope she will not launch into her familiar sermon on how to care for expensive shoes.

"Don't expect parents to keep all their promises," she says as she hears me come in. "Isn't that right, Dad?"

Her face is a study of conflicting emotions. Hope is dressed for winning a war: wearing a hand-woven skirt and an elaborately embroidered white blouse, with full sleeves, trimmed in thin red ribbon. She even wears makeup, a rare thing on a workday.

Frank looks back and forth at each of us, puzzled, but says nothing. His mother's dressing up for breakfast has not escaped his notice. If dress code determines the winner of the conflict, I have already lost.

"Your grandfather is contemplating a road trip across the country. I do not endorse this fantasy. Maybe you can talk him out of it." She turns back to the stove, stirring the scrambled eggs.

"What's across the country, Grandpa?" He rarely calls me that anymore.

"I have some old business to take care of, and I need to do it while I can still drive."

"Business!" Hope chimes.

"What business?" Frank wonders, "You have been retired for over five years."

"Personal, unfinished business. We don't need to get into details right now."

Nodding wisely, he says, "Oh that explains everything." Frank has inherited his mother's sharp and sarcastic tongue, which makes me chuckle.

"There's nothing funny about this, Dad," dishing up overcooked eggs, ham, and English muffins.

"I don't see any point in putting this off. I am leaving in a couple of days. There are some places in this country I have not had a chance to see, and I intend to remedy that."

"Like where?" My grandson is making polite conversation.

"Well, first of all, Oregon, then the mountains of Montana, maybe Little Bighorn, I'm going to play it by ear."

"Wow, I wish I could just take off and do that," Frank says.

Hope barely picking at her breakfast, visibly perks up, "I think that's a wonderful idea! Take a couple weeks off and go with your grandfather on this crazy trip. Maybe you can keep him from killing himself on the road. You can take the RV."

"Got too much work to do, Mom. Way too much work."

"Nonsense. I will buy the gas and talk to your editor. He is an old friend of mine, after all. Possibly you can send some of your articles from the road. This is a mobile society, isn't it?"

"Yeah, that's just what I'm afraid of. My job in the newsroom, there are others who are more than happy to snatch it up."

"We will talk about this at dinner. Please make it a point to be home tonight."

"Can't. Have a dinner date." Her son stops eating.

"Not anymore, you don't. Dinner will be at seven. Don't be late."

Chapter 4

*I have found that my soul cannot find rest on any
other path.*

—Debra Marie DeLash

John Goodwill and Frank
Hitting the Road
Santa Barbara, California

1 have always dreamed of setting out on the open road chasing
adventures. We should reach Oregon late tonight.

Frank, with the aid of his iPad, has mapped out our route
from West Coast to East Coast, locating RV parks and graphing
weather forecasts in states we will be crossing. He's just a little compulsive, like his grandfather.

After several rounds with Hope at dinner on why he must
accompany me on this "ridiculous romp through the country,"
Frank set aside fears of losing his coveted job. I have mostly occupied
myself with eating, letting my daughter get her son in line without
interference.

Bright and early at 6:00 a.m., we are both ready to go. "Hey, are
you coming, Grandpa? The day is getting away from us."

All of a sudden, *my* trip has been taken over and managed by my
young grandson, the organizer. Too much control is going to rain on
this parade. I wait on the enclosed patio outside the kitchen, while
Hope prepares our vegetable sandwiches and other mystery cuisine.
Frank prefers junk food, so her efforts may go unappreciated.

I may be the only one aware that this journey will end in God's
time, not mine, but will make it nonetheless. Does my daughter real-

ize that this may be a more permanent goodbye than my just taking a road trip? I dread Hope coming through the patio door, yet I want to get this farewell over with.

Hope walks briskly out onto the Saltillo tiles and hands me an overflowing lunch box and a leather bag containing important papers. The papers include a signed power of attorney with Hope's signature and mine, which assign medical responsibility to her, just in case. She takes her time, raising her eyes up to mine. Her mascara has become smeared.

"You know, Dad, I believe this whole trip to be a mistake. All this emotion cannot be good for you. Sometimes the past needs to be left right where it belongs, in the past."

I guess she may have figured out more than I thought. That's an annoying habit of children.

"I know, Hope. I know."

I have always been a self-starter, an entrepreneur who risked everything to start a new business, several times over. I call the shots exactly as I see them. Aging is a problem to be solved. Yet after the visit last week with Dr. McCain, I am forced to face my own mortality. Losing the illusion that I am always in charge is worse pain than the illness. I am battling anger, moment by moment. The memory of sitting in the doctor's office flashes by as I watch my daughter's face struggling to maintain composure.

I was clothed solely in a flimsy blue gown which exposed my backside, as the results of my chest X-ray were delivered with the MD's usual style, measured and swift. The only hint of his own stress was loosening his tie and unbuttoning his top shirt button.

"Irreversible lung damage. Increasingly resistant air exchange. In time there will be more and more difficulty getting an adequate flow of oxygen."

He let me take time to absorb this, saying nothing, dropping his eyes to give some semblance of privacy. A hushed minute ticks by, which seems like half an hour in which not a word was spoken. There has to be an answer to this, I'm thinking. I have to find a solution.

"I worked those years mixing concrete, probably damage from exposure to cement dust. No one wore masks back then."

I kept silent about the sixty years of smoking cigarettes. Fortunately, so did my MD.

"What is this resistant air exchange? If air cannot pass through my lungs, how will I function?"

Dr. McCain gently explained that energy conservation is important and to limit daily activities to the basics. It would take patience to adjust to the changed lifestyle. "Listen to your body, and your breathing. Don't ignore the impulse to slow down, take breaks and naps. No smoking, no drinking alcohol."

"I already quit drinking about three years ago. I just never bothered to tell you."

"Good for you. Now, all we can do is cross the next bridge when we get to it," he said.

If he thinks I can turn off the obvious message, and take baby steps through this, without thinking, he's nuts. I began putting my pants on, wanting to get the hell out of there.

"My lungs are damaged. That's what this damn report is saying?"

I don't think Dr. McCain would agree to this trip either if he knew. I saw no use in causing him unneeded anxiety by telling him about it.

An increasingly familiar ache in my heart brings me back to the present and my daughter. It is time to say goodbye to Hope. I reach forward and try to make our embrace relatively routine, not an extended farewell hug. The attempt fizzles, as I fight valiantly to stop unwelcome tears. Losing composure has never been in my comfort zone. In an attempt to protect Hope, I break the embrace.

"Drive safely." Her words echo as Frank pulls out the driveway.

Part of me wants to turn around and call this all off. Yet I know I couldn't really run away from this mission. I am almost out of time. I may not even have enough time as it is.

"Mom has the RV filled up, took over $300. Good thing she gave us a gas card."

I couldn't answer his cheery conversation but look out the side window lest Frank see me cry.

A memory flashes into my mind of when I was a boy and held a catcher's mitt in my hands. If I close my eyes, I can still smell the leather and the dirt at home plate.

There was my father, his father, and me: the long line of men in my family stretching far beyond a boy's comprehension. I recall, still with a boy's shame, the day I had screwed up in one of those baseball games and dropped an easy fly ball out in center field.

With razor-sharp clarity, I can still see the letdown on my father's face. The whole team laughed as I entered the dugout. Even my coach was disappointed. It had cost us the game.

Like a young warrior too young for the responsibility, I stuffed my tears and pretended to have some dirt in my eyes. I actually thought I could fool them.

Parents taught boys not to cry in those days. Mine was no exception.

"Boys aren't supposed to cry. You have to be strong," father would say. "You can't let anyone see your weakness because they will call you a sissy. No boy of mine is a sissy. You got that?" in his typical booming voice. He always seemed to be addressing the back row of the bleachers.

Frank and I had been on the road ten minutes, barely reaching Goleta when Frank's Blackberry buzzed loudly. He punches the button, and I hear monosyllables, "Huh, now? Right, Mom."

"That is Mom. She realized her spare laptop is in the bottom drawer of the bedroom. We need to turn around."

What seems a simple request brings me to my emotional knees. How can I withstand another good-bye when I am still recovering from the first one?

Hope is waiting in the driveway and quickly retrieves the computer. I just wave from the window, pretending to read my paperback.

Where did the years go? How can I let go of someone so important in my day-to-day life? I don't even know if going on this far-fetched journey will help. I glance back at my precious Hope in the outside mirror, as she turns and walks into the house with a final wave, her skirt swirling above her bare feet.

Wait! I want to call out to her, but she is gone. I didn't have the resolve to get out and follow her, grabbing one more embrace. I didn't think it would go well if I did. Neither of us knows how to deal with intense emotion.

Part of me longs to run after her into the house. I visualize closing the door to live out my days in comfort and security. I could close the door forever.

But to do so would be selfish fear. I owe a greater debt to my first daughter that must be settled. A glance down toward the thinning, weathered skin on my hands is a reminder the only time is in the present, and there is damned little left of that.

Is there truly hope to reach your destiny in your twilight hours? Or is it all too little, too late? Frank is pulling the RV out of the driveway for the second time, as I continue to question if this trip is a good idea.

"Young sir, I am ready. Put the pedal to the metal. We're losing the day."

All I can do is adopt a positive attitude and try to enjoy the journey without worrying about the destination.

Life is calling. It's never too late for second chances.

Chapter 5

*God knows our souls and fashions each uniquely; as
a key into a lock, we are made for a special purpose,
our mission. When we are obedient to our true calling, the key fits the lock perfectly, and we find peace.*
—Debra Marie DeLash

John Goodwill (Grandpa) and Frank
Cascade Meadows RV Resort, Central Oregon

"Hear the rivers are great for fishing, steelhead, and trout. Glad we are spending a full day here." Only someone Frank's age could be thinking about fishing at this late hour. All I want is to crawl into the bunk and sleep.

It is well past midnight, and we have reached Central Oregon. While Frank hooks up the RV, I make a cup of cocoa, sit down, and cross the first items off our eight-page "To-Do" list. With Frank's help, I have methodically created a recipe for destinations, places to see, and things to do. My main agenda, however, remains silent for the time being.

The sun rises beautifully to highlight a vast meadow with an awesome view of Mount Bachelor and the Three Sisters mountain range. I discover we are surrounded by over a hundred clear fishing lakes and endless miles of wilderness hiking trails in nearby Deschutes National Forest.

As I stretch my arms overhead to take in a deep breath of air without California pollution, I marvel at all nature offers in this amazing part of the world. Boy, it's good to be alive!

While Frank takes a hot shower, I attack the cooking duties. Thanks to Hope, our pantry is stocked with packaged breakfast meals, powdered milk, and canned fruits and vegetables. The plan is to eat breakfast and lunch in the RV, then enjoy dinner at local restaurants. Food just tastes better in the mountains. Gathering our omelets, muffins, and coffee thermos, we head to the picnic area.

"You boys looking for a seat?"

Three picnic benches await in our shared area between RV spaces. At one bench, there is obviously a newlywed couple, who prefer to sit alone. That leaves the two benches with a group of three men, a rather unique gathering who appear to have stepped out of a 1960s Peter Max lithograph.

Frank takes one look and turns on his heels to head back to the RV. I didn't think anyone could have spun on his toes so fast without breaking stride.

"How about a little wine or a root beer to go along with those muffins?"

"Sure, I'll take a root beer, please," I grin. Even though it is morning, I hear a corner of my alcoholic brain say, *Great, bring on the wine. I need it.* But I took the soda.

"Come on, Frank! There is room for us next to—"

A tall, lanky redhead with holey, faded jeans and a T-shirt with a bright red and yellow cosmic scene extends his hand in a gesture of friendship.

"Hey there, my man. The name is Sea Wind."

Frank turns around to join us, and I catch him rolling his eyes as I stuff a small plastic cup of wine into his hand. Hopefully, it will loosen him up a bit. I sit down between Sea Wind and Frank, not before, however, giving my grandson a warning look. Humor an old man, my look says. He sighs and nods as he sips his breakfast wine. I notice it is a California Merlot, and even Frank comments, "Nice vintage," nodding at Sea Wind.

"Come on, dude, chill a while," Sea wind says with a chortle that would put anyone at ease.

We tell him we are driving across country, to which news he nods smiling. He seems delighted with just about everything. I ask him, "Where you fellows headed?" Surprisingly, he launches into his history without guile or reservation.

Sea Wind was a child of undetermined parents. He spent his early years growing up in a number of Northern California communes and was raised by a kitchen sink variety of role models, a committee of surrogate parents who looked after everyone's children. He was a product of the so-called hippie generation from the 1960s and reports it was a wonderfully free and happy childhood.

"I was never told who named me Sea Wind, and finally gave up asking. I've gotten used to the raised eyebrows every time I say it," glancing at Frank with a huge smile. It is impossible not to like this young man.

My breath a little labored, I am relieved to meet this interesting group of fellow travelers and sit a spell.

"That contraption yours?" I ask.

I have not seen anything on the road like it in decades. Dumb question, as who else would fess up to that eyesore of a VW bus? Their home on wheels is painted on the side with bright golden stars, a ruby red sun, rainbows in shades of purple, and illogically, one domestic cat. I guess that the paint job resulted from a party, liberally fueled by jugs of wine.

"Yeah, that is our baby. I'm the mechanic who keeps her on the road." The rough-looking character who speaks is approaching forty years old I'd guess, a baby himself. His name is Joshua, which suits him, with the long black wavy hair, beard, and tattoos on his arms.

"Hey, guys, I'm David." The third member of this trendsetting trio is Asian, distinguished from the rest by wearing Native American buckskin pants and a flowered, Hawaiian shirt. He doesn't sit with us, but leans against the side of the bus, watching. He seems a bit leery of outsiders.

Frank is obsessed with the screen of his Blackberry, texting rapidly with someone, somewhere, about something unknown. I would have wished for better manners, but guess this is the best I am going to get.

I learn that the three men travel throughout Oregon, selling samples of their artistic talent. Joshua does weaving and sells an assortment of trendy baskets made from a blend of cane and grasses. David produces ceramics of a deep cobalt blue streaked with silver, in sets of dinner plates, cups, and saucers. All which they offer at various festivals and art shows on their selling circuit. Sea Wind is the musician clarifying, "Once we set up at a fair, I am supposed to attract business with my music. It doesn't always work, but I have fun doing it."

"If you don't mind my asking, Sea Wind, is it possible to make a living on this circuit?"

"Oh, you'd be surprised. People love art and craft fairs. They spend a ridiculous amount."

Seeing a sticker "Healthy Community Arts" attached to the side of the van, I ask Sea Wind about the name. He is eager to enlighten.

"We are a network, a team of street artists. We support many who life has thrown curve balls," Sea Wind explains.

"Like he says, we come together on art projects. We are here with each other and our communities," David chimes in.

Frank, by now, has finished his breakfast and chugs down the cup of wine. He looks up from his screen, asking, "You mean, you guys are like a mobile art gallery of sorts?"

Sea Wind has quietly gone into the van and retrieves his guitar. "When we are not on the road, I am a luthier by trade. I was taught as a child by a master luthier at the commune. I build and repair the guitars of the other musicians, and trade my services for food, sometimes a place to sleep for the night. I have also worked with violins, but I run into very few these days who play them. At least not in the circles we travel."

This time, Sea Wind didn't chuckle at the end of his sentence.

Sea Wind sits down on an old tree stump, about seventy-five feet from the picnic area, and is tuning his guitar and humming. He takes a deep breath and begins singing a Bach chorale, playing the complicated runs. He has a clear tenor voice, and it is a remarkable performance. When he opens widely, I could see he is missing a few top teeth in front. Yet he is proud to share his talent and tunes. It is about the music, not appearances. We applaud, and he nods his head in a modest bow.

"In answer to your question, Frank, you bet. We are a mobile gallery," David says, seeming interested in striking up more of a conversation. Frank isn't biting and annoyingly has returned to his screen. I look up at David and shrug.

He returns a friendly smirk continuing, "We are proud to travel to the various art fairs that will have us. In the van, we carry about thirty or so pieces of painted canvas. The best part is the fascinating people we meet." Still, Frank is quiet.

"Who does all the artwork?" I begin to be more than a bit envious of their vagabond lifestyle. I have spent my entire life working for "the man" eight to five, often six days a week. Isn't that what one is supposed to do?

Joshua pours another round of wine and hands me another can of soda. With the sun high up in the sky by now, we settle in.

David continues to explain, "Local artists bring their art, whatever medium. Sea Wind organizes everything, you know, provides tables, canopies, finds locations. We all meet up and have a chance to sell our stuff. We sell to businesses, people walking by, or to those who read about us in local newspapers and posters I put up around town. Then there are times we hit the road and bring as much art as we can fit into the van. That is, and still, have room for the three of us to sleep. Any money we make, we keep 30 percent of the sales to fund our street team, and the rest goes back to the artists.

"This art festival in Bend, we hope to sell lots of loot."

I figure this life on the road must be hard on keeping a job. I have to ask David, "How do you keep jobs with going on the road so much?"

Sea Wind puts away his guitar and rejoins our party.

"We receive funding for this project from our county's mental health division. The rest comes from private donations." Sea Wind is definitely not shy, and I enjoy his honesty.

"We are consumer activists and love what we are doing. We welcome all, and the emphasis is always on respect for the art. That is why we do it." David adds.

Sea Wind moves in closer and adds, "Our friend Joshua here, he started this gig. You know this old van, the work we have together, it saved my life."

My grandson is glancing up to listen occasionally, indicating he is a little more interested than before. I shoot a look which I hope reminds him to stay put. He has never been known for sitting still for long.

Joshua takes the last gulp of his coffee and tosses the cup into the trash can.

"Two points!"

Then Joshua begins opening up in a way not many men are comfortable in doing. He decides to share more about himself.

"I grew up different than other kids. I had a speech impediment, and my family traveled with a carnival. For various reasons, I just never fit in. As a teenager, I started hearing voices that told me to do things. They would call out 'Joshua' all the time. There would be messages only I could hear. Friends were people also self-medicating with drugs. We smoked anything, did acid. Nobody else would hang with us. I wasn't popular, rarely invited anywhere. I had to get stoned to stand people around me. In my early twenties, I had to admit something was wrong. I went back to the carnival where my cousin found me a job. But my thoughts were so much bigger than reality. They used to call me grandiose. I took off from my job, certain in the belief I was destined for huge accomplishments. I was always able to find work and make money, sometimes a lot. And I ran up debt. I ended up driving to California and was put in jail twenty days for vagrancy. They put me in isolation. The judge didn't know what to do with me. My mother came and flew me home to Oregon. I shot heroin in the plane's bathroom. Soon after we landed, mom took me for some kind of treatment, and a nice man played ping-pong with me. He also taught me about basket weaving. I still relax by weaving baskets today as you can see." It all began to fit, this van, the artwork, what the group is all about.

I start gulping down the third can of soda.

Joshua continues, "Eventually they prescribed meds to help. I started on Haldol, which took a while but finally worked. Except I had no energy or interest in anything when on it and tried to feel normal by quitting the meds. I had a couple of breaks when I would stop. I could see the expressions on people's faces as I walked into a room. They would whisper. I knew what was happening, and I could see what they were thinking, like floating messages in the air."

Sea Wind chimes in, "No one looks at us like that now. They identify us as artists."

It is making more and more sense. Frank even makes eye contact with Joshua as he finishes.

"My mom knew something was wrong but didn't know what," Joshua continues. "She would tell me, 'Joshua, you have to think good thoughts.' She would hold and rock me. Mom would keep telling me that for the rest of her life. Mom's words are the essence of my recovery. She told me to interrupt the craziness and replace the negative stuff with positive. My mom was a good soul and loved me. I would be watching TV, and she would see strange reactions in my expression. She knew something was very wrong. I would look over at her, and she would be crying. She didn't know what was happening to her son. But she never gave up. Mom always believed that I could learn to live with who I am. This recovery art project has set me free. I now have a purpose and a reason to quit trashing my body and stay healthy. Until I joined the group, I could not look anyone in the face. Now I feel free at last. I volunteered to organize the artists, and I haven't stopped since. I have learned from everyone else in the recovery movement. I stand now on their shoulders, in my imagination, in their spirits. Some are dead now, but I will always be grateful to them. I learned that my problem was not the bad times. It was the good times. I would get arrogant, moving fast, stepping on the toes of people who were contributing. I thought I was doing it all with no help. I would get busy, would not have time to acknowledge those who were also involved. I finally learned to take time to hear and receive. Through this fellowship with the guys you see right here, and others, I know that I belong somewhere. I am getting better, able to take care of myself, without having someone do it for me. It's a great motivator. There's nothing wrong with that. Most people think I am all about searching for love and feeling unworthy. But the fact is my lesson is to take care of myself."

David, who is now sitting quietly at the table, chimes, "And there is no real normal, is there?"

I thought about my own life and how much of it I have lived as a big lie. I wondered about my eighty-year-old self who sits here.

Am I but a mere shell of what is genuine and true? And who is really inside?

Sitting under the Douglas firs breathing Oregon air, and talking with these guys makes me feel younger, energized, as if there is still time left to make things right. These men have come out of hardship I have never known, yet they are more at peace in their own skins than many, myself included. I have even forgotten about my own health for a couple hours.

Frank in his impatience has resorted to pacing up and down the picnic area, so I decide to say my goodbyes and thank them for their hospitality.

Joshua and Sea Wind throw away our trash and head back to their van, as David warms up the engine. I wonder how many of their art pieces might sell at the festival tonight.

Their old van turns around and heads toward the exit. I notice the sign on the back door which reads, "Business _Not_ as usual."

As they pull out of the RV park for the first time in so many years, I laugh. I laugh so hard that I feel alive and love the feeling. I wonder where it has been. I have lived a life full of expectations, self-imposed, and otherwise, completely unaware of the invisible parallel lives I never recognized.

Chapter 6

We often keep secret our own mountains we must climb.

—Debra Marie DeLash

Grandpa and Frank
Hospital Detour
Sandpoint, Idaho

"We should hit Montana by dinner," Frank speaks with authority whenever information is verified by his smartphone.

Satisfied that he has posted our latest travel destination, Frank is ready to hit the road. I wonder how reality was ever verified before the days of Facebook. Early September and fall's approach, heralding the increasing chill as we head north, it will reach frigid temperatures before long in the northwest. According to the Internet, winter in Montana is not for the fragile.

The right side of my face is feeling strange, though I am still energized. After our breakfast with the artistic trio, Frank insisted on a two-mile hike in the Deschutes National Forest.

"Need to work off a few nervous vibes," he said. I waited in the RV.

We are heading north on Hwy 95, and I hesitate to admit I may be getting sick. Denial is a longtime friend, and I believe it to be a survival tool. Yet I know far too well what denial brings: an empty place, a vacuum, filled with "nots," not hearing, not seeing, not understanding, nor dealing with. Denial is not tangible or solid.

It's like numb. Numb does not feel pain, nor does it feel the absence of pain. Like denial, numb is emptiness.

For several hours, there has been this prickly sensation in my cheeks and forehead. I also notice soreness in my back whenever I try to speak. My efforts to talk with Frank are growing harder, and because I have to work at it, I slur a word or two. I wonder if he notices. I tell myself if I don't mention how I feel perhaps, it will disappear. After all, I have always been able to control my body.

Frank incessantly taps on the steering wheel to what I imagine is a favorite tune in his memory. The constant motion of his hand is driving me nuts. An approaching sign announces US 95 North. In forty-five more miles, we arrive in Sandpoint, Idaho. I have never been there, not sure I want to now. The last fifteen miles stretch on forever as I begin to perspire.

Finally, we cross a bridge over Pend Oreille Lake into the town of Sandpoint. I am not in the habit of watching for hospital signs, but today I spot the blue capital "H" on the road.

"Get off at the next ramp, South 1st Ave."

"What? Why, Grandpa?"

"Follow that blue sign. Yeah, let's see, take this left on Cedar. Keep going. Now, take the right, here on North 3rd."

"This is a hospital. What are we doing? This will throw us off schedule."

"Frank, I need to see a doctor. I am not feeling well."

Frank seems surprised and annoyed. A young fellow of twenty is not used to medical interruptions, I suppose. He stops by the entrance to the emergency room and asks if it would be okay if he meets me inside.

"I need to, uh, be right back after I park." He seems uptight, but I have bigger fish to fry.

I amble into the emergency clinic and can only hope I am overreacting. Boy, do I detest this medical stuff. After leaving my ID and medical coverage cards at the intake desk, I sit down under a sign that announces *triage*. Once the kindly nurse takes my pulse, temperature, and blood pressure, I am escorted inside the emergency room without the customary wait time. Not the best sign. She starts an IV and hooks me up to what looks like ordinary saline.

The doctor who ordered every test under the sun finally returns and pulls the curtains shut. He clips an X-ray of my lungs onto the lighted screen. It all looks like the normal grey and black, except for two small patches of white on the bottom.

"Looks like you have a little something in your lungs. Have you had pneumonia recently?"

"Three weeks ago. Treated with penicillin, rested for a while, and I have been up and about since."

"What about breathing? Does it seem labored?"

"I don't know about labored. I stop and rest every so often, but I do all right." I already knew my lungs are damaged, so I thought okay I get it; now let me out of here.

"Sir, from the looks of the CAT scan, you have had a TIA."

"What the hell is a TIA?"

"It stands for transient ischemic attack and often may go unobserved. The issue is TIAs may be a sign of an impending, more serious stroke. Have you noticed any facial weakness? The right side of your face is a bit droopy, though I don't know you well enough to be sure. It does look a little better since you arrived here around... Let's see."

"Four hours ago!" Damned hospitals. "When can I get out of here?"

"I'd like to keep you for observation. I started medication in your IV to thin your blood."

Right about the time I ponder between cursing the gods for this news or ripping out the tubing and running out the door, Frank returns. He appears incredibly chipper compared to the grumpy fellow he was when he dropped me off.

The kindly doctor explains to Frank the reasons his grandfather needs to stay overnight. Frank, content with the medical assessment, turns toward me.

"Seems like we are here until tomorrow."

I feel control over my life slipping away into alien hands and annoyed, begin to panic.

"This TIA, this mini-stroke, has passed, and I am feeling much better. Listen, no more slurring, I can even smile with both sides of my face."

"Where were you headed when you came in here?"

"Through Montana, all the way across the north to Maine," Frank announces.

"And we want to get going," I tell him firmly.

"I understand, sir, but we need to keep you overnight for precaution. You are headed into Montana mountains, and there will be little to no medical assistance available out there should you require it. You really can't gamble with your health. We will continue the antibiotic drip for twenty-four hours while monitoring for signs of another TIA. I also want to talk with your own MD in the morning."

Oh, drat! Now I suppose I have to explain about my trip and wait for the shoe to drop. This is going to get sticky. Frank chimes in before I can open my mouth.

"My grandfather and I are heading on a road trip across the country. A bucket list so to speak."

This thirty-something doctor hesitates a moment and then shakes his head. Realizing I am outnumbered between Frank and this overly zealous doctor, I have no choice but to let the very large orderly wheel me into a hospital room.

Chapter 7

*Faith turned sixty years old this year, and I wonder
absolutely everything about her.*

—Debra Marie DeLash

Grandpa and Frank
Hospital
Sandpoint, Idaho

Mornings begin early in hospitals as the white-uniformed staff rev up their engines. There are lives to be saved in Bonner General Hospital, Sandpoint, Idaho.

After setting up the Skype call to Hope, Frank has taken off to the cafeteria for some of their muddy coffee brew. I don my gray tweed sweater to hide the IV line, attempting to tone down the traditional hospital garb. Hope doesn't need to be unduly alarmed by what she sees on her computer.

"Dad. How are things going?" She's wearing gardening clothes, and her hair is a bit messy. I'm hoping this is only a minor interruption in her day, and there will be no theatrics.

"Good morning, dear. How is the garden coming?" I hurry on without waiting for a response.

"Oh yeah, Frank and I are fine. We took a short layover here in Idaho before we head into Montana. There are beautiful puffy clouds in the sky today."

"Mr. Goodwill? Oh sorry, you are on a call."

Drat these nurses, always pushing pills or taking blood pressure. The nurse loudly announces, "Sorry to interrupt, but it is time for your breathing treatment."

Nuts, now I'm in for it.

"Dad, what is happening? Where are you?"

"Now I don't want you to make more out of this than it is. I was a little short of breath, so we stopped here for a couple of routine tests. They would have called you if it had been anything unusual."

"Came where? Are you at a hospital?"

"Just a lingering symptom from my previous pneumonia, that's all. I am told these strong antibiotics will clear it up. By tomorrow, out go the tubes and off we go."

"Put Frank on the line," Hope barks.

"Sorry, dear, I can't. He's downstairs in the cafeteria. Which he would not be if there was something to worry about."

One thing I hate about these high-tech calls is being able to see who you are talking to. Where is the privacy?

"Something about this doesn't ring true," Hope continues.

"Dear, please remember I am a grown-up, not your child. Really, I am merely following hospital protocol. You know how hard it is to make sense out of their procedures. An old guy walks in here, and they figure I must require a tune-up. Anyway, these days they probably need the business. This place is almost deserted."

"Dad, it is time for you and Frank to come home."

"No, dear, it is not! I can't turn around now. Heck, Frank and I are almost in Montana. Maybe you can fly out and join us? We can all go together."

I sigh and wish this could be true but pray she will refuse. I would never get away with continuing this trip if she were here.

"Are you losing your sanity? Dad, you are not well and need to be home. Fall is on the way. I really don't want to imagine my father and teenage son caught in an East Coast storm."

"Dear, when we hang up, go online and Google the weather for Montana. You will see how beautiful it is up there. You know I have to do this. I have imagined starting out on this trip so many years, and now the time has finally come."

"What? Risking your life to chase after a daughter you hardly know. How do you even think you can find her? Clearly, Dad, this is a mistake."

Hope's left eye twitches every time she experiences stress. This Skype call shows my daughter's disapproval in living color. Is this progress?

"As I told you, in the morning, Frank and I are heading east on Hwy 200. This takes us into Montana and toward a little town, Thompson Falls. Lovely this time of year as AAA boasts on their Web site. I hear the Clark Fork River is-"

"Knock off the travel log, will you? Does Frank even know about the destination of this crazy scheme?"

"Crazy scheme? Would you care to rephrase that, dear? I can't imagine you would tolerate such disrespect if I were to speak to you like that. I'm saying goodbye now, Hope. We can Skype again in a couple of days."

Frank returns with the coffee as I close the computer screen.

"What was that about?" Frank is only mildly curious.

"Your mother is in a mood. Best leave her alone for now."

*****

It is a fitful night sleep as a result of nurses coming to take my temperature and oxygen tube adjustments. Dawn is finally announced by a tall, blonde-haired man sporting a name tag introducing Dr. Nebund. He looks as if he has been up for three days straight. I politely listen to his sermon on my various medical maladies and how he is not comfortable with discharging me. He says something about oxygen saturation levels.

I tell him that is fine, but I have someone waiting for me, and I flash a happy smile to cover the panic that they won't let me out. He looks confused and a little unnerved. He is unaccustomed to back talk from patients. After all, *he* has an *MD*, and *they* don't.

As if he expected my protest, Dr. Nebund pulls a form out of the chart called "Release against Medical Orders," and hands it over. After a moment of hesitation, I scribble my name quickly, lest his thoughts linger any longer than needed.

The choices I make stare back in the mirror. I only did what my father told me to do as a man. Why does everything seem at odds with what he taught? Where did I go wrong?

As I grew up, I tried to do the right thing as my father had defined it. I married the mother of our baby. Though only nineteen, I thought that age was filled with adult wisdom. I was wrong. I attended night college and entered the business world.

I remember my huge pride when we brought our daughter home from the hospital. I vowed to my twenty-year-old self to set the world on fire. I would provide for everything my wife and child needed. Life is going to be great!

Those sunny days of our Faith's early childhood became lost in a world of overtime hours and client networking. My wife navigated through years of temper tantrums and behavioral interventions at school, all essentially in my absence.

When our daughter screamed there were monsters in her room, I instructed my wife, "Let her scream. Children must learn to be strong." However, the crying would go on for hours until she finally wore herself out. I would get so frustrated. I kept thinking I had to keep our family on track. But I was losing control.

During our daughter's middle childhood years, I largely ignored my wife's fears. When she cried that our daughter was not well, something was not right, I thought she was being overly dramatic and increased my hours away from home.

Then I began to drink. I had a long commute, and I would unwind with pop-top cans of wine in the car. It was the planet's worst vintage, but I didn't care. It was medicinal. I had to be settled down before I walked into the zoo that was home.

My young wife cried day and night over the one we love, who was showing early signs of mental illness, our cherished daughter. I was expected to provide strength and answers. But a mentally sick child had not been the script I had imagined. My head was always spinning.

One night as I approached our front door after a long day, I heard them both crying. In the pit of my stomach, I had to face the fact that we were in trouble. All I could do was to keep breathing and focus on control. I crouched in the front yard grass, pulling dandelions for over an hour before going in.

Our daughter was almost fourteen years old, and my wife was already exhausted. Neither of us understood how our little girl could have changed so severely.

My reflection in the hospital mirror forty-five years later is a reminder that the past is in the rearview mirror, the future is very iffy, and the only time I have is now. My *now* is about finding my daughter, Faith.

I check inside my wallet to make sure it is still there. Folded and tucked behind the picture of my current family is a small envelope. Up in the left-hand corner is printed the name James Cannon, Private Investigator. I reach inside and feel the comfort of the worn, index card showing the vital information I need. Faith turned sixty years old this year, and I wonder absolutely everything about her.

Faith lives in a small town on the southern coast of Maine. Before I moved in with Hope and Frank last year, I had collected all I would need for this long-awaited journey.

When we are in the throes of a life-changing decision, as I did so very long ago, we tell ourselves half-truths. Before running away to the West Coast, I convinced my younger self I was leaving Massachusetts for a short time only. I will clear my mind and escape the madness. I will sort out the myriad of feelings and return stronger than ever.

What intervenes to stop our well-laid plans and dreams? Life happens. We live from moment to moment, putting out fire after fire, just surviving. Before we know it, there is an eighty-year-old face staring back at us in the mirror. Who let that stranger into my life?

It is never too late to make a difference. I just hope Frank is willing to humor this old geezer and keep driving. I have stapled together Faith's contact information and the name of the hospital in her Maine hometown, just in case.

Chapter 8

*Life is about the journey. The destination comes all
too soon.*

—Debra Marie DeLash

Grandpa and Frank
Montana

After Frank picks up my medication from the hospital pharmacy, he finds me waiting in the lobby. I cannot be sure, but I wonder if Hope talked to Frank last night. He seems more restricted, borderline sulky. I will do my best not to scare this young fellow with medical dramas any further. We fire up the RV and head out of Sandpoint, eastward on Hwy 200. Look out, Montana, here we come.

We ride in silence for an hour and a half, each with only our thoughts for company. This may be the longest period of quiet I have ever witnessed from Frank. I let the dead air hang, waiting for him to speak. We are heading east on a road through a long valley shared with the Clark Fork River at the bottom and high snow-covered peaks at the top. The roads are winding, merely two lanes, with various animals: whitetail deer, elk, and large squirrels. Watching for animals darting out from the trees reminds me how quickly we can be in trouble, how this life can shatter in minutes. Along the highway are white crosses put up by the VFW to honor road fatalities.

Majestic trees appear everywhere, and I believe the phrase, Montana is God's playground, to be accurate. Close to lunchtime, Frank pulls into the Thompson Grille and breaks his reserve.

"I'm going to die if I don't get something to eat. Are you hungry, Grandpa?"

"Good grief, yes. I've had nothing but that awful hospital food."

Thompson Falls is a small town roughly over a thousand population. We pass the Sanders County Courthouse on the main street, along with a vintage movie theater, apparently closed. Unexpectedly, the little Grill is brimming with activity, and at first, I do not find a place to sit.

"You men looking for a seat? You are welcome here. My name is Sharon."

I look around and spot a woman about sixty-five years old with very short gray hair, tan, and motioning to us from her booth. She scoots over and allows me to sit beside her. Frank rolls his eyes and takes the seat across as I thank her for the courtesy.

Sharon starts the conversation, "Thompson Grill is *the* social gathering locale this time of year. Within a couple months, winter will hit with a vengeance. Then most people stock up and stay home. When cabin fever takes over, we crawl in along back roads to the Grill. It depends on how severe and how long the winter months are. This past winter wasn't really bad, no sub-zero temperatures, but it seemed to go on and on.

"About the only amusement in winter is church on Sunday and the bookstore across the street, Barely Read Books."

"Oh, that could get a bit depressing, being homebound and all. Are you from these parts, Sharon?"

"Wish I could say I am, but no, I relocated here from Vancouver, Washington, after my esteemed friend passed away a few years back. Looking for a place, I suppose, to escape and write my memoirs. And learn to fish."

Frank pokes his head up from behind his Blackberry to take a bite of the bison cheeseburger, which has arrived at our table. "These are the best fries I have ever had," he announces happily, "What's their secret?"

"Oh, they won't tell me. But you're right, they spoil you for any others." He appears a little curious about this mysterious woman. She sports the most fabulous bone Native American choker around her neck.

"What is your book about, Sharon?" Frank asks as I gobble down one of the tastiest sandwiches I have had in a long time.

"First, might I ask what brings you gentlemen into our fine town?" Sharon sure seems to know her way around talking with relative strangers. I find her friendly spirit a pleasant surprise.

"We're just passing through on our way to the East Coast," Frank replies.

"Now that you mention it, Grandpa, we should be hitting the road soon. I'd like to put in another seven hours before setting up for the night. Need to make up for lost time."

"Oh, nonsense," Sharon boldly interrupts. "You must visit the National Bison Range which is only an hour from here. I would love to show you the Oreo cattle and their babies. This has been quite a prolific season for babies of all species. A Canadian geese couple has produced twenty babies which you may see, along with another couple who have fourteen teenage geese."

My grin widens at this rare opportunity for an up close peek at nature's finest. As I pay our tab, Sharon explains we may hook up our RV at her friend's motel on Maiden Lane, which runs along the riverbank. Maiden Lane was so named for the ladies in the early 1900s, who made their living in small cottages there.

"The larch trees are visible now, turning golden brown before they drop their needles. In the spring, they emerge as soft lime green, almost like baby hair. This will be fun. I have never had the privilege of showing visitors Montana before." Sharon seems to sense my grandson's growing restlessness.

"Hey, life is about the journey. The destination comes all too soon, Frank. If we head there directly, we'll be back by nightfall."

She's clearly not about to let us miss this rare sight of Native American bison roaming the hills. I wonder how much credit Montana air and trees whispering in the wind receive for her inner calm. Frank shows concern, but I am more than a little intrigued about what Sharon may share about her life's journey. Heck, I could use a little peace and some diversion.

When I point out to Frank this rare photo opportunity and how he could post marvelous pictures on Facebook, he reluctantly agrees. As we pull out of town, sure enough, we pass a riverfront park where the Canadian geese and their babies are grazing on the lawn.

"So now tell us about your memoir, Sharon," Frank reminds her.

"Well, it's a story of a nightmare childhood, with alcoholic and inattentive parents. It's not a story that is in style with the rotten economy, so I self-published it on Kindle. The second book will prove more interesting, I think. Aside from an assortment of failed marriages, it centers on the dying process from pancreatic cancer. My ex-husband died four years ago, and our daughter and I took care of him."

"That sounds like an awful ordeal," I say, feeling great pity for what her family went through.

"Yes, and no," Sharon says. "I have come to realize in the peace of Montana's mountains that it may have been one of the most blessed experiences I have ever had."

"I don't understand," Frank replies.

"I know, and that's the sad part. Most people will run as far and fast as they can to get away from the dying process. And that is an awful mistake."

"Can you explain?" I turn in my seat to watch as she continues.

"Sure, but you won't believe me. Neither my husband nor I were very good at intimacy, sharing deep feelings, understanding each other. But when he was dying, he relaxed and opened up, and so did I. Every morning when I would come on duty to care for him, he would tell stories of his childhood, and years in college. I took notes in shorthand, and when he would fall asleep, I transcribed his words onto the computer. He would ask what I was doing, and I said I was going to write about him, and he was delighted. On the day before he died, he asked, 'Do we have any unfinished business?' I told him we did not, trying not to cry, as I knew he didn't have much longer. We both realized that we had found a deep friendship that we never had when we were married. It was perhaps the greatest gift I have ever inherited. It sounds very strange nor is this popular, I realize, but helping someone you love through the dying process is an experience to be sought, not run from. You will be grateful forevermore if you allow yourself to follow the narrow path."

Chapter 9

Every sunrise embraces the adventurer, the dreamer,
and we mere mortals, who continue to hope.
—Debra Marie DeLash

Grandpa and Frank
Driving through the Dakotas

As we head out of Thompson Falls the next morning, I feel these old bones perking up a tad. Frank and I both slept like the dead after our trip through the bison refuge and cattle ranch tour. It is partly the fresh air in Montana, but there is more than that. I realize that Sharon's story came at the perfect moment. It is time to be honest with Frank, and I pray he can handle the news. He's a bit young for the dying journey, but time is shrinking, and we need to get down to business.

Frank has our itinerary mapped out with an unrelenting path across the continent's Great Plains. First, we will drive through North Dakota, which has a new claim to fame, that of "fracking," extracting oil out of shale. It is a dangerous process, and the controversy over the damage done to the environment is in the media, but one has to search for it. We then move on to South Dakota and land with a stopover in a Nebraska KOA. With many hours ahead of dusty flat roads and little interesting landmarks, it's time to open a more meaningful conversation.

He makes it easy to begin by asking, "Isn't Sharon's story fascinating?"

"Yes, you're right, and it makes me realize that there are some personal things I need to share too."

And so I begin to tell my story.

"I haven't said much about this whole road trip. Heck, I reckon I don't say much about anything. At least about things of the heart, the things that really matter. It was not an acceptable conversation when I was a kid, and to this day, it's very hard to break those rules of silence."

"What are you talking about?" Frank replies. "You've always made sense to me. I just mean, well, the day with Sharon, outside of all the beautiful photos, it was quite a shift from any day I can remember. First of all, a total stranger shares her life. And she seems very content with where she is. And I don't mean her surroundings, though they are gorgeous."

"I know what you're saying," I respond. "For me, it's mostly about finding myself at eighty years old somewhere I never thought I would be. It has happened just like that, a blink of an eye sort of thing."

"I hardly think about your age, Grandpa. You hold your own."

Words of encouragement like that from the young always indicate to me that the subjects of old age and dying arouse nothing but head-in-the-sand denial. They are overwhelmed, cannot face it, so they insist on telling the aging that they will live forever. We know it is crap but can do nothing to stop it.

At Frank's tender age of twenty, of course, he wouldn't dwell on the deeper processes. Like this seemingly endless highway in front of us, life is an illusion. I thought it would extend out in front for a long time too. And it did for a while. Then, one day, I woke up, and here I am trying to believe I'm the same man or close to the same. But try as I have, I know that the various MDs have given fair warning. I need to discern reality from denial. If I am going to leave this life with integrity, things must get harder before they get easier. As my sponsor in AA says, "The only way out is through."

"Frank, I want to tell you why this cross-country trip is so important."

"Go ahead, but don't go get too serious, okay?" He turns his glance in my direction, and I know he means those words.

Generations of men denying their feelings, demanding numbness from all their descendants: "Men don't cry!" echoing from their graves. If a man is careless and lets an emotion sneak in, he must immediately dig a hole and bury it. I have to explain this to a young man whose genes thrive on denial, as hothouse plants drink in Miracle-Gro. He's going to have to grow up fast.

"As you know, son, I have always worked hard. Heck, I am the only one of my friends who waited to retire until seventy, and I still dabble in real estate. Take Ted, he couldn't wait to leave his dentistry practice at sixty-two. He spends his days on the golf course and horse races. Matt, well, he likes to play farmer on his small ranch up in Santa Ynez Valley. Never watered a tree in his life, and now, he rides up and down his vineyards wearing overall blue jeans and a brimmed straw hat. All he lacks is a corn cob pipe."

Frank chuckles at the image, and the speedometer needle moves up to seventy-five.

"Let's try and make the Nebraska border by 8:00 p.m. What do you say?" He is evading the subject, and for the moment, I allow it.

"You are the conductor of this baby. Keep moving out, Frank."

I sigh. I have spent my life trying to outrun my feelings. As we all know, and some of us will even say aloud, none of us will live forever. But even though I have signed a living will, watched my late wife succumb to cancer, and heard the grim news from my own doctor last week, I still try to bargain with God.

Admittedly, on some level, I don't want to believe I am really going to die. But that nagging voice where I imagine my courage lies won't shut up. My twelve-step program tells me to say the Serenity Prayer when things get sticky. Frank must accept that our trip is no longer an optional one. He needs to know I am sick, and come hell or high water, we need to get to Maine in time.

"You ready for a little lunch?" Frank shines his impish grin. He pulls over to a rest stop and heads for the galley. After preparing a simple meal of turkey on rye, with canned fruit cocktail and a few gingersnaps, we sit back in our front seats.

"As I started to say, my friends all had a vision of how their retirement would be. They worked for the day when life could be relaxing, unstructured, finally having time for themselves."

"All that relaxation is not for you, Grandpa?"

"I never could stop making deals. Buying and selling became a way of life, always has been. Now I realize that being driven has been to my detriment. I could never face slowing down."

"Umm, yeah." Frank washes the last bite down with his fancy sports drink. Noticing my breath is becoming more strained, I stop and deeply inhale in between bites of my sandwich.

"Our time with Sharon, though a bit intense, changes my perspective, Frank. That's all."

"What do you mean? I find all her talk about dying quite depressing and not a topic for vacations. This is all about fun!"

"Frank, stop. Listen to what I have to say. I am not as healthy as I may look. My lungs are weak, and I have several blockages in my heart which need attention."

"Attention? You mean surgery? Then why the hell are we on this desolate road?"

"I am telling you this not because I want to go back home. I am telling you for the sole reason that I *must* forge ahead no matter what and need your help to get this mission completed."

"What does Mom say? Wait! Does she even know about this heart stuff? I am not a doctor, but it sounds like this is something you need to take care of sooner, rather than later."

"I need to get to Maine. My time is running out."

"Does Mom realize this? What is so important?"

"No, and I don't have time to deal with her objections. Right now we need to haul ass and get there fast."

"What the hell am I supposed to say when she calls?"

"You stall, say we are hitting traffic, and you can't deal with conversations right now, something like that. Keeping things from your mother is surely not new territory for you."

Frank blushes and mumbles, "Yeah, I guess I can do that."

The road stretches wide open, and I quite shakily drop the second half of the bombshell, the one that we are heading to Maine to find my long-lost daughter. After my explanation, Franks falls very quiet.

I feel as if I just ran a marathon. My feet are numb, and I try to wake them up by doing range of motion exercises in the seat. Could my surfacing emotions increase my physical problems? It just can't happen. It's not time. Overcome with fatigue, I recline the seat, prop my head with a pillow against the window, and collapse into a deep sleep.

In my half dream state, I can hear the loud clanking of keys as they entered the lock of the inpatient psychiatric unit forty-five years ago. I see again my daughter's legs twitching incessantly along with the rhythm of anxious fingers as they scrape at the hollow of her neck, drawing blood. I feel the terror resurface as I try desperately to make eye contact with my young beloved, searching for any hint of connection on her face. So many years have passed, yet the dream is in full bright colors of a scene so long ago.

As the sunrise beckons a new day, blasting light on my face, I awaken to Frank's quietly humming "Bridge over Troubled Water." After my bombshells, he had said little more and has driven all night while I slept. He glances over, and looks unusually vulnerable, a bit skittish.

"Were you able to get some decent rest sitting up?"

"I should have gone back to bed, but I was too tired to move. Thanks for not waking me."

"Grandpa, what is your other daughter's name?"

"Her name is Faith. I have not seen her since she was fifteen. I left because I was too immature to deal with her mental illness. Now I have no more time to hide from my responsibility. It's probably too late, but I have to try. Frank, I have run from unpleasantness all my life. I'm in a battle with shame and regret, in addition to a battle for my life."

"I can't tell you, Grandpa, that I understand it all, but you must know that I will do anything I can to help. I think we had better send Mom an e-mail, at odd hours, so she doesn't want to Skype. We have our hands full. Let's try to reach our stopover by tonight," Frank explains, popping a couple yellow caffeine pills into his mouth.

Each day is a new beginning. Every sunrise embraces the adventurer, the dreamer, and we mere mortals, who continue to hope. As long as there is a breath in this worn-out body, I will awaken my spirit and reach the only goal God-willing, worth fighting for. Every mile brings me closer to dear Faith and what I hope is my personal redemption.

The remnant of time I have, the only time that really matters, is framed by every remaining breath I take as we tear east on the freeway toward my first daughter.

Chapter 10

*One does not expect such drama from the inside of
an RV.*

—Debra Marie DeLash

Grandpa and Frank
Pine Grove RV Park
Greenwood, Nebraska

After driving a couple of uninterrupted days, the scenery
begins to lose its attraction. Frank suggests we pull over and
get some sleep before we begin to babble and drool. We are
quickly approaching the west border of Iowa and southward where
we will stop at the Pine Grove RV Park in Greenwood, Nebraska.
Frank is holding something back, and though I would have rather
kept driving, I realize even young people need a little rest and relaxation. Maybe he will be able to open up and say what's on his mind.

It is late afternoon as we pull into the Pine Grove and decide
on a spot near the swimming pool. In early September with temperatures in the high 70s, the pool is open and busy. I see a horseshoe
pit and think maybe after a good night's rest that might be a healthy
diversion. We pay the fee and hook up.

I am amazed at the services available; this is not your grandfather's RV park. There are wireless connections everywhere, even in
the bathroom. I also spot volleyball and tennis courts, an exercise
room with modern showers, and a convenience store with a café.
Frank and I decide on the café for a simple dinner and then to bed.

Since my no-holds-barred conversation about Faith, and why
I must see her, Frank seems a little distant. I sense he feels as if he is

carrying the weight of the world on his shoulders. At his age, it is a pretty big burden. Once we settle into our booth, Frank pulls out his Blackberry and scours the Internet for distraction, which he shares while we eat.

"Hey, Grandpa. Here are some Nebraska fun facts you might like. There used to be this crazy law on the books that donut holes may not be sold in Lehigh. Or what about this one? In Omaha, sneezing or burping during church services is illegal."

Frank downs the last bite of apple pie, lets out a big burp, and laughs loudly.

"Arrest me, anyone?" he says. This time I have to laugh, and we both begin to relax as we lose ourselves in unrestrained, abandoned giggles, partly fueled by road fatigue.

"Gramps, did you know Nebraska is the birthplace of the Reuben sandwich? And there is a law somewhere that you cannot sleep naked in a hotel room? Try enforcing that one!"

We find ourselves laughing so hard, I barely notice the young man who is sliding his chair closer to our table.

"Love the smell, don't you?" Frank and I look at each other, silencing our chuckling long enough to address this twentyish, tall, and thin lad now in our company.

"What smell?" I ask, after performing the niceties of a brief introduction. Apparently, he isn't interested in names. He has other priorities.

"The marvelous aroma of freshly baked waffles and hot maple syrup, indeed," as his eyes nervously dart from our booth to the café entrance and back.

Realizing there are no waffles or hot syrup in sight, I am a bit confused but to each his own. Frank slams down his techie device and turns to our visitor.

"Hey man, what's up? Quite a few travelers for September. Where are you traveling to?"

"I had to leave in a hurry," he begins. "Folks back home, man, they think I am behind a string of convenience store robberies. Can't go anywhere, the movies, arcade, park, even downtown. They whisper behind my back. Even the kids stare as if I have a disease. Happens everywhere. Getting tired of it, you know?"

At this point, I am staring at him too and allow Frank to solve this puzzle.

"What do we call you, my friend?"

"Why do you want to know?"

"Well, it makes conversation easier, I guess. My name is Frank. This is John Goodwill. To me, he is Grandpa."

Instinctively, Frank senses the young man's need for boundaries and does not extend his hand. The nickname Twinkles comes to mind as he possesses the most sparkling, emerald green eyes imaginable.

Suddenly, Twinkles pushes his chair back over the black and white linoleum tiles, causing me to cringe at the fingernail across a chalkboard sound. The dozen or so folks in the small café look our way, and this is all it takes.

Apparently, in response to an imagined threat in his confused mind, Twinkles leaps up, prances backward, waving his arms in the air, as if fending off attacking insects. He begins to shout nonsensical words. As Frank and I watch, stunned, several of the men stand up and come toward Twinkles in an attempt to help, which may or may not be what is needed.

"Stampede!" Twinkles yells and runs toward a corner table with a red checkered tablecloth, probably there since the 1980s. There is a centerpiece which, unfortunately, happens to be a lit candle. I cannot restrain my fear of impending disaster.

"Someone blow out the candle, damn it!"

The rest of the patrons are just sitting there, with quite a few mouths open in disbelief. I have to do something; I grab my flannel coat from behind the chair and bring it toward Twinkles, who by now has crawled under the table. He is cowering on the cracked tile floor, shaking in his private and mysterious anxieties.

"Here, put this on, young man. It will protect you, really."

Carefully on my bad knees, I crawl under the table and sit down next to him. I place the oversized coat around the thin, terrified youngster. I am surely a hundred pounds heavier than he, and the coat envelops his body twice over. I pull it around him and pat his shoulder through the heavy coat.

I feel Frank nudging my leg. "Come on, Grandpa. Let me help you up."

"We're quite comfortable down here, Frank, aren't we?" I look at Twinkles, and he nods his head solemnly.

The waiter has run out of the café to find Twinkles's parents, who are outside hooking up their RV. Thankfully, the commotion dies down as Twinkles's mother and father come back into the café to retrieve their bewildered son, who crawls out from under the table and placidly follows them out the door.

By now, I am back in our booth catching my breath and trying to calm down with a steaming cup of hot cocoa on the house. In a couple of minutes, Twinkles's father approaches to return my coat and thank me for helping his son.

"What is going on with him?" Frank asks, not mincing any words.

"Jeremiah. My son's name is Jeremiah," he says, pulling off his glasses, rubbing his eyes. He's exhausted and slides into our booth. I look at him and immediately get it: a father's heart. There is no escaping his pain.

He turns to me and says, "His diagnosis is paranoid schizophrenia with the dreaded psychotic features." I nod silently. Someone just walked over my grave. After a few moments of sympathetic conversation, I am relieved when he says goodnight and heads out.

In silence, I close down the café that evening, drinking hot cocoa, unable to get the father and son out of my mind, there but for the grace of God. Is this the life I would have had if I had not run away from my daughter, Faith? My heart splits between guilt and relief. My legs refuse to move until long after midnight, when I finally head back to sleep, needed much more now. Frank has already been dozing. Perhaps whatever is on Frank's mind will be allowed to surface tomorrow when we hit the road again.

Only one other RV still has their lights on, and I notice at the window Twinkles/Jeremiah and his parents are still awake. Jeremiah is talking, with grandiose hand gestures toward his parents. They have set up on the spot next to ours. I feel guilty to realize how grateful I am not to be his father.

This will be no ordinary journey for that family either. When we see an RV on the road, we only visualize vacation and fun, which was Frank's fantasy of the trip. One does not expect such drama from the inside of an RV.

Chapter 11

If we have the compassion to offer a second chance to others, isn't it time we offer it to ourselves?
—Debra Marie DeLash

Grandpa and Frank
Pine Grove RV Park
Greenwood, Nebraska

My eyes open to the sound of laughter outside and the slow realization of where we are. I awake unsettled, from dreams colored with faces vaguely familiar, yet unnamed, and endless twisting and turning passageways to unknown destinations.

A quick glance around the RV shows Frank is up and gone. These old bones could use a jump start; I just need some caffeine, and I'll be ready to venture to whatever awaits. I slowly put on my plaid wool shirt and decide on the comfy sweatpants. At my age, who cares about appearances? Dressing seems to use up more than enough energy.

As I finally open the door, there is a fragrance in the air, of something blooming I can't identify. It crosses my mind to stop, close my eyes, and try to remember the fragrance as long as I can. The thought flits by that I will have fewer and fewer of these moments.

I carefully descend the steep RV steps and walk over to join the small group playing horseshoes. Twinkles's dad stands behind his son, attempting to instruct him in the proper grasp of a horseshoe. It looks like dad has already checked for accurate measurement of the stakes at forty feet apart and explained the rules of the game to his son, along with any passersby. Somewhat compulsive, I'd say.

"Hey, good morning, all. Has anyone seen my grandson Frank? I slept in and am just wondering—"

"Oh, sure. We saw him heading down toward the clubhouse about an hour ago. He seemed very preoccupied."

I couldn't help but see how Jeremiah, or Twinkles as I call him, would calm down when focused on the game. He tosses the horseshoe toward the stake and hits it. As a beginner, he has amazing and unexpected eye–hand coordination. He smiles and glances at his dad and then at me for deserved approval. He appears to remember me favorably from last night's interlude under the café table.

"Mind if I join the game?" I cautiously ask. I believe horseshoes is a game almost anyone can play, even this old man. The requirements are pretty simple-minded: you have to stand up, toss the horseshoe toward the stake, and hope it at least hits. If you are lucky, it rings the stake, and you can smile as Twinkles did.

"Sure, here you go." Twinkles hands me a horseshoe and steps aside.

"Thanks. Let's see. When I used to play years ago, we scored three points for a ringer, two for a leaner, and one for a square away."

"I'm cool with that." He shines his gleaming pearly whites, and I silently grieve that his mental disease may steal away this charming young man's future.

"It's been a lot of years. Let's see if I still have it in me."

"There you are, Grandpa. Sleeping Beauty finally woke up." Frank has returned from the clubhouse and slams his phone down on the picnic table, letting out a lingering sigh.

Twinkles says, "I'll go stand on the side of the sandpit and bring back your horseshoes. I feel better when I am on the move."

Twinkles hands a shoe to Frank, determined he will play. He looks a little annoyed but takes it.

"Okay, Jeremiah, let's see what this old geezer can do!" I take a deep breath, lean forward, and throw with all my might. Horseshoes are heavier than they used to be. It falls short of the stake by about eight inches.

"That was just for practice," the boy says. "Now do a real one." We look at each other, and then I toss a "real" one.

"Way to go! A leaner, two points."

Twinkles threw his hand forward to high-five his dad who has joined his son on sandpit duty. Full of exuberant energy, Twinkles retrieves the horseshoe and runs it back to me.

"Thanks, young fellow." I turn toward Frank. "Your turn."

Frank looks like he would rather be anywhere but here but humors his grandfather and hurls the horseshoe. He misses the stake completely, hitting the sideboard surrounding the sandpit. Definitely distracted, his heart just isn't into this. Twinkles, who is increasingly revved up, runs to grab the horseshoe and returns it to Frank. Frank throws again and hits inches from the mark.

"Square away. One point your way, Frank."

We continue our game and Twinkles becomes a virtual whirlwind with his running back and forth. He seems to feel the simple joy of the activity, as does a puppy chasing a ball tossed over and over. With all the bending and stooping, my breath becomes short, yet I am having fun seeing Twinkles so engaged and, for the moment, without fear. These moments of success for him may be rare. I find the energy for one final shot. My one-boy cheering section yells with such delight; I am sure he can be heard in Iowa.

"Presto! Ringer! Three points! Looks like your grandpa takes the game, Frank."

Twinkles appears as proud for me as he would be for himself. He runs up and hugs Frank with one arm and me with the other, making it a three-way group hug swaying to and fro. Laughter is contagious, and even Frank joins in. Does it ever feel good to let loose, losing the haze of impending doom that has followed since my Idaho hospital visit. Suddenly, I feel a need to get back on the road. Time here has been golden, but the clock is ticking again.

"Frank, let's get moving. What do you say? Let's put in some miles."

Frank, more than agreeable, says, "Okay, Grandpa!" as he heads over to unhook the RV.

I approach Twinkles and his dad to say goodbye and ask, "Where are you folks headed?" A nicety I prefer a quick answer to, thank you.

"Oh, out toward the San Francisco Bay, California. The Amen Clinic. After all my research into brain illness, I believe this is the place that can help Jeremiah."

"Okay. Well, safe travels then, and good luck."

I extend my hand for a quick handshake.

"Right. I am optimistic about Dr. Amen and his theories," he continues.

Darn that compulsive nature of his. I just want to get going.

"You see at the clinic, they will scan Jeremiah's brain and iden-tify any specific areas which cause problems. By seeing exact regions where the brain lights up, we can better target treatment. I see a lot of promise, don't you agree?"

"Of course, I'm sure your research has brought you to the right course of action," I respond, hoping this ends the discussion.

This detailed, scientific-oriented father obviously did a great deal of study, and I applaud him, but it is time to go already. I turn around and because by now I am more than a little lightheaded, I neglect to notice the stake in the ground directly behind my heel. Damned if I don't trip and fall clumsily to the ground.

"Jeremiah! Call your mother!" Twinkles's dad barks. His son quickly runs to their RV and up the steps, yelling, "Mom, come quick!"

I'm sitting on the sand feeling foolish, and before I know it, I am being helped up by a rather round, gray-haired woman, who escorts me into their RV. She walks with purpose, plopping me down at her kitchen table. In no time, she becomes nurse matron whipping out professional equipment to take my pulse and blood pressure and even using a glucose meter to measure blood sugar.

She offers a glass of orange juice, which reminds me I hadn't bothered to eat breakfast. I obediently gulp down every last drop while she watches.

"Your blood sugar is only sixty-five. No wonder you are dizzy. Do you often get like this?" Twinkles's mother sits down and begins to make a list of all my medical numbers, ignoring the fact that I have not answered. "Your blood pressure could stand to come down a bit, too."

Standing in the doorway, Frank asks, "Should I call Grandpa's doctor?" I suppose he is jumping to the conclusion that I am going down that dark road this minute. I hate this whole process. All I want to do is get out of there and resume driving. It's time to bargain.

"Okay, listen up everyone. I did not eat breakfast, played a little too hard this morning without coming up for air, and yeah, I am not as young as I used to be."

A plate of reheated waffles and eggs appear.

"Thank you for your kindness. I'll eat this lovely breakfast and promise to rest. But we really must get going."

Twinkles appears from the back room to join us at the table. We eat in a worried, stale sullenness interrupted only by the sound of Twinkles clicking his fork rhythmically against the plate. After a moment, Twinkles's dad mercifully interrupts the clanking and speaks, "If you men are intent on hitting the road, at least let me put together a list of hospitals on your path. You know, this has saved me these past years with Jeremiah's illness."

"Don't get him started on my illness, *please*!" Twinkles jumps up, drops his plate into the sink, and escapes out the door. As his mother begins to talk, I hear the sound of a horseshoe hitting the stake.

"I hate mental illness," Twinkles's mom sheds her nurse matron attitude and reveals a broken mother's spirit. "When Jeremiah received his diagnosis of schizophrenia, I already knew it. I spent years sensing something was awry. It wasn't long before the early signs of psychosis shattered our daily lives. One day, I came home to find he had shut all the curtains in the house, was holding a large butcher knife in his hand, filled with terror that we were all being attacked by aliens. I called the doctor, who referred us to a psychiatrist, who immediately admitted Jeremiah to an inpatient hospital for the mentally ill. This was the beginning of, well, all of this."

She points to a rather large stack of printed articles, an assortment of pages ripped from various books, and a blue, plastic basket full of prescription bottles. I recognize an old, familiar feeling in the pit of my stomach. Stuffed beneath the surface all these years, I don't have time to let my pain, frustration, and heartache explode.

Twinkles's dad continues on relentlessly with facts, due in part, I suppose, to keep his own pain at bay.

"I have studied extensively, current research, medication trials, and treatment protocols. Our mental health system is failing terribly. Do you know our prisons are housing many of our mentally ill? So many of the homeless are alone, hungry and scared. These are today's faces of mental illness."

I should understand what he is living through. But I have lived my life trying to avoid facing the very same things they cannot avoid. His mother continues, "I am so scared that one of those faces will be our son's someday. How does a mother live with that?" There are unrestrained tears coursing down her cheeks.

"Why don't they get treatment? Can't the families put them in a hospital? There must be something to be done," Frank asks.

Twinkles's parents look at each other and hesitate before answering.

"Young man," Twinkles's dad begins.

"Call me Frank."

"Frank, one of the dastardly parts of this brain disease is that the person may lack awareness of their condition. They don't see a need for help, not understanding they are sick. They will insist all is fine and everyone else is blind."

His mother continues, "Even if they do consent to go for treatment, funding is poor, psychiatrists are few, insurance is nonexistent or very limited. Then the medications have side effects many refuse to put up with."

The more Twinkles's mom talks about his illness, the more she seems to age before my eyes. I see on her face what every day, every year I have run away from. I am watching the toll mental illness takes on the loved ones.

I finish the last bite of eggs and quietly put my fork down on the plate. My heart is beating faster, reminding me to breathe slowly, evenly. I turn toward Twinkles's mom and say something I never dreamed I would, to a complete stranger.

"Long ago, a different lifetime really, I loved someone with a mental illness. It started out with noticing a series of idiosyncrasies, inappropriate social behaviors. My wife and I tried to help our daughter. We took her to doctor after doctor. She was in her teens, the symptoms increasing daily. The doctors had difficulty reaching a diagnosis, finding the treatment to stabilize her."

"Where is she now?" Twinkles's dad asks.

"I had to keep the family going. There were bills and I had to keep a roof over our heads while this drama played out. I buried myself in my job, worked overtime, and admittedly, there were nights I didn't want to go home. I am not proud of that."

Beads of perspiration are forming on the back of my neck. My body must not fail me, not yet.

"To answer your question, we are headed to Maine to find my daughter. I have had little contact since she was a teenager. My wife and I divorced after I moved away. Now I need to see how she is, what her life looks like."

"And, if by chance you don't like what you find, what then?" Twinkles's mom gently puts her fingers on my pulse and looks me in the eye. "In my opinion, you need to be under medical care, not traveling the country in an RV. Why now, why not leave it alone?"

"Yeah, sir," Twinkles's father says. "Why do you want to do this to yourself?"

They get some truth and a little evasion, "For love. No one may believe this as I did abandon her and all, but I never stopped loving my Faith."

"Grandpa, you did the best you could back then. You have a new life now. You've had this life for forty-five years, right?" Frank has trouble comprehending a timeline that long and just wants the problem to go away.

"No, Frank. My duty was clear, but I had not the spine to do it. My wife would lie in my arms and cry until exhausted and asleep. I had to be the strong one. My father, all the men in our family, was raised to not show emotion. Men didn't talk about things like mental illness or anything to do with family problems. Around the water cooler at work? Men bragged about their son's home runs or

64

their child's medals for honor roll, stuff like that. I had no one to talk to about my daughter's illness. Those were the days before social media."

"Men still don't talk about this stuff," Twinkles's father explains. "I know if it wasn't for the mental health online groups, I would be isolated with all this."

I feel a kinship with these people and open up a little more.

"I remember the feeling of walking in this world all alone. Soon I began to talk to women, who seemed to understand or were more inclined to talk about mental illness. Other days I would focus on anything that was *not* a mental illness. It had taken over any life I had dreamed of. Of course, that turned out to be a mistake. You see, I feel no peace with the choices I made."

The familiar urge to escape returns, and this time I vow to be different.

I cautiously stand up and look toward the door. This conversation is fine and all, but stirring up this talk only helps if I can make things right. I put my arm around Twinkles's mom and offer a hug. She leans her head on my shoulder for a moment, then pulls away.

Almost on cue, we hear Twinkles's creating quite a stir outside with the managers, ranting and raving, something about tornadoes and imminent doom. Twinkles's parents run out of the RV to rescue their son from irritated men, who are beginning to shout back at him. I pick up the list of hospitals Twinkles's dad has methodically created for my benefit, left unfinished on the table.

Frank looks like he is ready to explode. "Grandpa, there is something I need to talk about, but it's just for your ears. Let's get moving. It can't wait any longer."

I realize it is time to leave Twinkles and his family behind. After all, I have my own family who needs me, and I intend to be there this time.

"Definitely, Frank. Isn't that what grandfathers are for? I'm at your disposal."

I could almost feel generations of men in my family rolling in their graves as Frank fires up the RV. I nestle into my copilot's seat and ready myself for whatever Frank needs to say.

One of the things I love about this life is we are given chances to repair our mistakes. If we have the compassion to offer this second chance to others, isn't it time we offer it to ourselves?

"Head on out, Frank. Next stop is Illinois. We have some miles to cover, and nothing is more important today than what is on your mind."

Chapter 12

There comes a time after the storm, when we realize with eyes wide open, what we have done.
                                                    —Debra Marie DeLash

Grandpa and Frank
Iowa

Alas. The gift of time and we only have the now. Why is it that when we see life slipping away at lightning speed, this lesson becomes so clear? Does the illusion of immortality create our blindness? Frank and I cross the line into Iowa heading east, and I fight to stay awake. The days are ever so slowly shortening as fall is fast approaching. It is 7:00 p.m., and the road ahead is dark.

I must dig deeper with a fierce determination and battle a lifetime that has become expert-level shame, all the wasted energy trying to fight my own demons, reconcile my sins, and seek forgiveness. My mind goes back and enters a simpler time when the world was my oyster. I remember sweet Sarah, Faith's mother, and our brief happy years together.

Sarah came from one of those families that happy 1950s TV shows are designed around. People watch reruns on cable channels with their kids and grandkids. Love of the innocent characters is timeless. Sarah had read *Adventures of Huckleberry Finn* four times before she graduated high school. Her other tattered and worn literature were Judy Blume books, which her parents approved of somewhat less than Mark Twain but tolerated what they considered an excursion into junk food for the mind.

Her family had various branches of aunts, uncles, cousins, grandparents, and in-laws. The extended family lived on contiguous hunks of ranch land in Wyoming, with the exception of a "rebel" older sister who escaped to Massachusetts when she married a traveling salesman. Sarah said at the time this was quite the controversy. The family land totaled around four hundred acres, which was considered relatively modest for eight families.

Sarah was petite, with thick, curly red hair; her skin tended to freckle in the sun. All her cousins went to a school eleven miles away and were picked up by the bus, which was filled with family. Sarah often spoke about summer days spent swimming with her cousins in their pond. It was natural, with cattails along one edge, lots of frogs, salamanders, and those amazing little "skates" that scooted along the surface tension of the water. All in all, it was a blissfully happy and unsullied childhood. Sarah's parents never traveled, and so she thought that this part of Wyoming was the real world. What was on TV, cities, and other countries where people spoke strange languages were about as relevant and familiar as Mars.

It wasn't until she was sixteen and her father died that she found herself plunged into a brand new world. Her mother got a job through her sister, and the family transplanted into Massachusetts. She would be an administrative assistant within the Boston legislative offices. Sarah's mother bought a house there, and Sarah found herself surrounded by more sophisticated teenagers in a new high school. I met Sarah as we walked into our first class, junior year.

I remember her look of awe at my clothes. They came from expensive stores and looked nothing like her family pool of hand-me-downs. I was attracted to the warmest smile I had ever seen. From day one we were inseparable.

Some of the girls tended to look down their noses at the "Wyoming cattle kid," but I found her simple, earthly qualities endearing. Sarah enjoyed going to the parties at big houses with exotic food, not just meat and potatoes. And since she was pretty and new, the boys buzzed around Sarah, like bees around the hive. As soon as I noticed this, however, I asked Sarah to be my steady girlfriend. I couldn't have been happier.

Sarah's mother thought that Boston was not a bad town for her daughter to find an appropriate husband, one with potential and future affluence. Since Sarah was the youngest of five children, her mother was ready for an empty nest. When Sarah became pregnant during our senior year, both my parents and Sarah's mother agreed we should get married. And we were happy to abide by their wishes.

Our daughter Faith was born five months after our small church wedding.

I can't help but think to this day maybe, just maybe, if I had stayed with Faith and Sarah; if I had been stronger, I might have done more to help those I loved. It is impossible not to venture into all the different scripts that might have emerged if I had chosen differently.

Would they have been better, or perhaps worse?

Freud said, "There are no accidents." So was I part of Faith's path, even Sarah's, by my leaving, or did I cause incurable damage?

Can I teach Frank anything and turn things around for this next generation? If he takes my advice, will that balance the scales? I put a halt to my mental reminiscing and turn to my grandson.

"Okay, young fellow. You seem like a person with something on your mind."

"Yep, I have a problem all right."

I wait for Frank to continue, but he apparently doesn't know how to begin or to overcome his resistance. It's genetic, this running from awkward emotion. I'll try to help him out.

"Well, I notice your distraction, times you slip away, and the phone calls where you return visibly upset. I know something is going on. You can talk to your ole grandpa. Mum's the word. I would never repeat anything to your mother, or anyone else."

"Yeah, I suppose I do. There is a little situation which is bothering me." Again, I wait and bite my tongue. After an eternity, maybe ten minutes, I can't stand it and open my mouth.

"Spill the beans. I know we have not spent much time together, but I am here now. I have seen a thing or two in my days. Go ahead and spill it."

"Well, uh, let's see. There is a girl. A girl named Dawn," he begins.

"Okay. Continue please, son."

"Dawn and I graduated from high school together. You were at the ceremony. Remember the girl who came to our dinner afterward, at the Miramar?"

"The petite, blonde beauty? She came with her parents, didn't she? Sat across from your mother and me, only down the table a bit."

"Right. We have been friends most of our lives. Our parents are friends. We grew up going sailing as families, summer trips to Catalina Island."

"Sounds warm and fuzzy all right. But I imagine there is more to this story, right, Frank?"

"Yup. There always is a kicker. And I have the mother of all kickers."

I couldn't help thinking why don't these youngsters speak English, but I know we also had our own way of talking back in the day. I best keep my mouth shut and eyes open and alert, no easy task, as it is close to midnight.

"Go ahead. The night is young."

"Grandpa, I love Dawn. We started going out a few years ago, pretty much an exclusive sort of thing. She is the only girl I have cared about. At least so far." Frank lets out a little chuckle, and I wonder how deep he has stuffed his feelings.

"Is Dawn who you talk with throughout the day? Sounds like a love story, and yet, I see something else in your eyes. What is it?"

"I don't know. I mean, this is all so hard to talk about."

"Of course it is, Frank. We are men. We are supposed to keep our struggles, our choices, heck our feelings inside. Nowhere do we learn how to talk about inner workings, as I call it. Believe it or not, I am fairly new to all this myself, being candid about personal things that were always considered private. For me? I am safe talking about work, sports, anything besides that ache inside my heart. I am only guessing here, but I bet you are running away from something that brings you pain. Take it from this old geezer." My resolve to keep my mouth shut is slipping away.

"It's just, I mean, I can't put Dawn out of my mind. Take this trip. Each mile we drive farther from Santa Barbara and Dawn, the worse things seem."

I know Frank is holding back, and it is time to steer his course.

"Boy, can I relate to you. Forty-five years ago, I packed my earthly belongings in one large suitcase and headed out in an old Buick from Massachusetts to the West Coast. Part of me prayed the car would break down and I'd have to return home. But the bigger part wanted to escape and find a happier life. Since marrying my high school sweetheart, then having Faith get so sick, I was overcome. God help me, but I longed for simpler days. I thought I could forget the pain. Now I know this was a delusion. It forced my choice to leave and completely change direction. But even now, if I relive my debate over whether to stay or start fresh in California, the pain is right there. Time never made it easier. You see, stuffing my story away all these years did not make it disappear. Keeping my truth, the past hidden, not talking about it, not dealing with it, I have not had any peace. I want better for you, Frank. So talk."

"I failed Dawn when she needed me the most, Grandpa!"

"You are on the phone constantly. She is still an important part of your life, isn't she?"

"Now? I can barely live with myself. Every morning when I open my eyes, I think this will be the day the memory fades. I made a terrible choice. It eats at me day and night, following me with each mile."

"Yeah. I get it. Know what you mean."

Frank continues. "When I talk to Dawn, she is a reminder of how I screwed everything up. I was faced with a dilemma and what did I do? Took the coward's way out. I see that clearly." Frank begins to sniffle, fighting tears.

"Pull over, Frank. Up ahead, that's it, park under the old olive tree."

We had driven all night. Barely 7:00 a.m. and we are only thirty minutes away from Springfield, Illinois, and our scheduled stop. Frank turns off the ignition and reclines his seat. The sun is rising from the east, and though physically I feel exhausted if ever there is a time to persevere, this is it.

I cannot help but notice how worn my hands appear as they reach behind to unbuckle my seat belt. There is just enough space to carefully, slowly lower down onto my knees and reach over to embrace my grandson. My breath is labored with the effort, but I want with every ounce of my being to be exactly where I am.

Frank hangs his head and continues to grip the steering wheel though we are parked. If he feels awkward that I intrude on his physical boundary by crouching nearby and placing my closest arm around his shoulders, he doesn't say anything. He seems frozen by accumulated emotion, but the dam is breaking.

Frank begins to sob, and his tears flow from a deep place inside of my own heart.

*****

Frank's heavy breathing in and out, fighting unfamiliar tears, triggers my own memory. I softly tell him my story.

"The bedroom in our tiny 1960s Massachusetts apartment was decorated in bright yellow. There was our bedspread with vibrant embroidered flowers, shutters with matching material weaved through every row of wood panels, and canary yellow walls. My young wife decorated with such care, as she did everything in our lives.

"Our rebellious daughter was fifteen years old, restless, find-ing fault with everything her mother and I did. One day without warning, Faith picked up her earthly belongings, stuffed them into a denim sack, and ran away from home. It had been three eternal days when this particular evening, she finally called. I picked up the phone from the bedroom.

"Faith had ended up in Portland, Maine, roughly five hours north of Boston. Apparently, a woman who lived on the streets took Faith under her wing, and in a psychotic state, herself created the perfect storm for a father's torment.

"My young wife was spared the details of the phone call that fateful evening. I, on the other hand, heard the words and felt the daggers reach my soul. My dear daughter, the one I worked for and loved, was convinced by this street woman that I was the devil incarnate.

"I don't remember the exact words or arguments she used to convince me of my evil. I could tell that in her mind she really believed her father was to be avoided at all costs and that she would never come home.

"This memory is so vivid. Even today, I can smell the aroma of the bacon frying in the kitchen. My wife in a hurry to come to me had forgotten to turn off the stove, and the bacon burned. I remember the feeling of my young wife's velveteen pullover sweater against my bare forearms. Soft and luscious, yet of no comfort. There was nothing that would lessen the agony of my daughter's words.

"Even today, I cannot describe it adequately. The tradition of burying emotion was stronger than the need to break down and grieve over the magnitude of her hateful tirade. Back then, uneducated concerning serious mental illness, all I knew was it hurt way too much. I hung up the phone as a friend who was visiting came into the bedroom.

"At that instant, I simply wanted to die. Against everything I was raised to do, I exploded into a torrent of tears onto my wife's shoulder. This time she was the comforter, holding me in her arms, sitting on that bright yellow bedspread, as she rocked me back and forth as she would a baby. At first, she asked, 'Sweetheart, what on earth is wrong? Nothing can be that bad.'

"I remember crying so hard and tasting the salt of my tears for hours afterward. At one point, I recall opening my eyes, meeting the gaze of my friend, who stood in the doorway, watching in horror. I closed my eyes again, closing them both out of my pain.

"I eventually pulled myself together, and we called the Portland Maine Police. They managed to find Faith and returned her home. Delusional and suicidal, Faith experienced her first admission to the inpatient unit at the Boston Psychiatric Institute for a seventy-two-hour hold.

"Yet I was never able to forget the intensity, the heartbreak when my dear daughter thought I was the darkness. And I never recovered from the moment when visiting Faith at the hospital, my own father arrived and called me a failure. The guilt was so overwhelming. The next day, I got in the car and just drove.

"It took years to realize my relationship somehow ought to be with my daughter, and not with her illness. But by then, I had met and married your late grandmother and became a father again, this time to your mother. It was too complicated to imagine fusing the two disjointed lives together. I chose to deny my past and begin anew as if I could just erase that time of life."

Frank had been crying silently, his shoulders shaking as if he is fighting what is happening. Could his pain be as much about the shame at crying as it is about Dawn? He finally speaks, his head buried in his arms against the steering wheel.

"Grandpa, I made Dawn have an abortion. I talked her into getting rid of our baby. Now that is what I call a failure!"

I hold Frank close as his sobs increase uncontrollably, loudly. My gift is the freedom to allow his pent-up emotion to finally burst.

"I feel so guilty. I can barely look at myself in the mirror."

He pulls away slightly, and I realize my right leg is cramping as I slowly manage to stand up erect.

"When did all this happen? Your mother, none of the family had any idea you were dealing with such a crisis." I shake my head knowing that ever since my daughter's divorce from Frank's father, the family is fractured. Everyone went off in different directions, with communication limited to distant phone calls and Christmas cards.

"I have been too ashamed, Grandpa. I kept this whole thing quiet. I had found an upscale clinic in West Los Angeles. It took weeks to convince Dawn that we could not keep the baby. She wanted to consider adoption. But I guess I wanted a fresh start. And truth be told, I didn't want to have to tell anyone, especially mom. I thought it would all just go away."

"Go ahead, Frank."

"I paid cash for the abortion. I drove Dawn to the clinic and convinced myself I was being supportive just by being there. We rode down Hwy 101 in silence. The Pacific Ocean was glistening in the sunlight, but neither of us noticed. I thought her subdued mood was due to the Xanax the doctor prescribed to calm her nerves. I can see now that the medication was more to quiet the voice inside which wanted to scream.

74

"I sat in the clinic waiting room the entire time. My mind was in total disconnect from my heart. At one point, I thought I heard the sounds of a girl screaming. I could have sworn the voice belonged to Dawn, but I shut it out and tried to concentrate on an old copy of Parents magazine. For such a momentous event, it took very little time. I was shocked when they told me she was ready to leave."

Frank's tears are gushing down his cheeks. I reach over to pull his head down onto my shoulder. I realize how much I love this boy.

"There, there, son. You are not alone."

"I am responsible for this terrible loss and pain. How will I ever live with myself?"

"Son, you will learn to live with your past, as we all do. Anyone who feels no mistakes on his conscience is a fool. If you don't know it already, I want you to learn the Serenity Prayer. You will find it is your greatest tool when things become too much to handle." Frank nods, gets up from his seat, and enters the kitchen. Barely awake, I know we both must sleep. He returns with two cups of hot herbal tea.

"Frank, it's a short drive to Springfield. Tell you what, it has been a long night and a hot meal prepared by a professional cook, no offense son, and a king-sized bed sounds mighty good. Let's find a Marriott and park this baby for a much-needed rest. My treat. We'll be fresher and can head out first thing tomorrow morning."

"Sure, good idea. I don't think there is anything left in me, except to shut down for a while in sleep. I'll put these away." Frank places the NoDoz pills back into the drawer on the dashboard.

"Think I'll just head into the bedroom and get a jump start on that sleep," as I hobble toward the back of the RV. My breath is troubling. Just tired, I hope.

"Thanks, Grandpa." Frank pats me on the back. I turn around and face him squarely as he asks, "Will this regret ever go away?"

"I wish I could tell you I know how life will turn out. What I do know is you being able to tell the truth about your experience is a pretty good start. Do you know how many folks invent a different version of reality? Tell themselves a different story so they can live with things. You, young sir, are way ahead of this trap."

"Hope so. Think I'll head back to the ole wheel and get us to that hotel."

In the remaining stillness as I drift to sleep, I feel compassion for this young boy who is just starting out. He has so much ahead of him, and I realize something I never have before. Without a doubt, who Frank really is as a person will not so much be about what his actions were in the past, but what he learns from this experience, and where it takes him from here. The content of his character will determine his future.

I believe for the first time, I get it: who we dream and commit to being will define our true character. We will make mistakes, but what we learn from them will constitute the building blocks of living authentically with ourselves and with those we love, even if our time is running out.

Chapter 13

I can still hear the doctor announce, "It's a girl," as he lifts her up into the air. Every moment since then pales in comparison.

—Debra Marie DeLash

Grandpa and Frank traveling toward Indianapolis, Indiana

The night at the Marriott proves refreshing for Frank, evidenced the following morning by the bounce in his step and relaxed smile. Perhaps the moments of honesty we shared in the RV were cathartic, and his plan to reach out to Dawn is easing his wounded conscience. Oh, the possibilities of second chances.

I, however, am not as resilient. The moment I crawled between the fine cotton sheets, I lost consciousness for nearly ten hours. Morning should have found me somewhat rested, yet I am still as tired as when my head hit the pillow. Immediately, upon standing up from the edge of the bed, I notice an irregular heartbeat pounding in my chest. Time for the deep-breathing exercises from my physical therapist. At this point, Maine is roughly a two-day drive, and I am definitely not sharing my state of physical not well-being with Frank.

"Look at these gas prices, almost $4.00 a gallon. I remember when prices barely topped eighty cents. Highway robbery!"

Frank grins and tops off our big tank. After over half a day on the road, we cross into the state of Indiana. The dark skies look threatening, and there appears to be a storm rolling in. Internet service is rocky, and I instinctively want to find a real newspaper. I wonder if Frank has ever seen one.

"Let's pull over at the Quick Stop ahead. The one with the line of fire engines, see? Wonder if this place can provide us with a newspaper."

"I don't know, Grandpa. Not many places sell those anymore. It's a virtual world, you know." I can imagine his mind equates this with the horse and carriage.

"That's true. I just feel like I need to get the current news and hold it in my hands. I miss those days."

"Oh sure. Let's give it a try."

Frank pulls into the store, and still feeling short of breath, I decide to wait in the RV. He returns carrying the familiar newsprint, though a bit thinner than I remember in days past. One of the firemen walks over to Frank.

"You guys from these parts?"

"No, sir, from California. On our way toward New England."

"I reckon you didn't hear. Storm headed our way. The further east you go, the worse conditions are."

"Storm? How bad? Tornados seen in these parts, March through August. It's past Labor Day," Frank speculates. "Thought we would miss all that."

"Mother Nature. Temperamental at best. Of course, state weather service posts emergency updates on local stations. But the storm is gaining strength past couple hours. We're on tornado watch throughout Indiana. Looks quite unruly toward Indianapolis."

"But that's the direction we are headed."

He hands Frank a brochure on tornados, action plans, and a list of local shelters.

"This list is fresh off the wires. These shelters are accepting folks. Whatever you do, don't get caught on the road, young man. A tornado will pick this RV up and toss it clear to Sunday."

I roll down my window and stick my head out.

"Excuse me, but my grandson and I really need to get to Maine. How certain are you, I mean is there a chance we can get through? There are no confirmed tornados yet, are there?"

I can see the fireman glance over to Frank and roll his eyes. Not a good sign.

"Son, take your grandfather and get to one of these shelters. The first one, Mercy Shelter, is only a mile south. Better safe than sorry. I'd hate to be picking up pieces of you in some wheat field."

"Yeah, thanks," Frank gets behind the wheel and hands over the shelter list.

"Those young firefighters appear a bit anxious. They mean well, and I know better than to try and reason with their protocol. Frank, let's keep moving forward and get through Indiana. There are no tornados right now."

By this point of our journey, and not feeling well at all, I am taking life one step at a time. Pulling out the map from the glove compartment, I figure we are only six states away to the finish line. A sense of urgency is overcoming my usual reliable logic.

Frank pulls up the Internet on his trusty Blackberry and shares his newfound knowledge.

"Let's see. There's a difference between a tornado *watch*, which is what this area is under, and a tornado *warning*."

"Go on, what does it mean? Can we keep going?"

"Give me a chance, okay. The tornado watch covers all of Indiana, which we crossed into an hour ago. Tornado watch—large hail, damaging wind threats, in addition to tornados. Seems bad, I don't know. We might be lucky to only experience wet weather."

"Well, how long do we need to worry about this so-called watch? Who is stirring up this concern anyway?" I knew I was sounding irrational but was unable to let go of my personal imperative.

"Let me see, Grandpa. Storm Prediction Center says three to eight hours."

"By then, we can be in Ohio. I am going to lie down. Wake me if road conditions get worse. And the point is, as of now, there are no tornados to worry about."

"Are you feeling sick? I mean, wouldn't hurt to pull over and spend the night." Frank takes one look in my eyes, shrugs his shoulders, and fires up the RV.

My sleep is restless, partly caused by the uncertainty of the days ahead, and knowing I do not feel ready to die. I've never been much of a spiritual person. My relationship with God is mostly reserved for an occasional Sunday mass. Every time I leave the church, however, there is a part of me that simply feels lost. Maybe church services reach some people, but I always feel I am pretending to be something I'm not. I suspect my guilt gets in the way; to lose Faith remains a big part of my soul. What happens to people who pass away and carry such a burden of guilt? I guess I'll find out, won't I?

The ferocious winds blast against the small bedroom window, the rhythmic banging trashing my nerves. It's like a two-year-old playing with grown-up drums. I pull the blanket over my head and try to roll on my side. The dead could not sleep through this racket.

We travel another hour or so before the clouds break open like Niagara Falls. Frank slows down in response to the torrential downpour. As I sit up in bed, once again my heart is pounding, accompanied this time by dizziness. "Focus, breathe, and don't panic!" I remind myself. After sitting up and deep breathing for close to fifteen minutes, I decided to test the waters. Slowly, I stand up erect. Whew! I am okay.

My right leg is a little weak as I shuffle up toward the command station. The storm is blasting the windshield, and I wonder how Frank can see. The wipers are at full speed yet not helping, the RV now rocking in the strong wind.

"Grandpa, we should pull over. I know you want to make Ohio, but this is freaking me out."

"I don't know. We are so behind schedule. I just want to get there, that's all." Again, I am being irrational, and the thought that I am endangering my grandson creeps in.

"I need to say, mom has been checking in twice a day. She is worried about you. Maybe she is right to worry."

"Yeah?"

"You know I am on board but look out the window! I am barely able to keep on the road! These things are so top-heavy. We could tip over. Grandpa, we need to take a break. I am pulling into the next motel. We are only ten miles out of Indianapolis. I don't want mom finding out we were swept away by a twister into the land of *Oz!*"

I have to turn away. I can feel the tears leaking from my eyes.

"I am scared that I am going to die on this damn road. Please do not talk to your mother, or anybody else. Let's make a run for it."

I resume my copilot seat, and Frank reluctantly continues toward Indianapolis. By now, the RV is swaying side to side. The road signs are few and far between. I retrieve my reading glasses as not to miss any information. Slowly, I walk over to the desk, and that moment is when I see it.

Franks computer screen is always turned on and connected, as the young folks put it. Bold as can be and plastered on the screen in bright red is the following announcement.

"Tornado warnings issued by the local National Weather Service for Indianapolis will remain in effect between 6:00 p.m. and 8:00 p.m."

It is now 7:00 p.m.

"There is trouble brewing, son. I think you are right. Get us to a shelter, fast!"

"But, where? There are shelters in Indianapolis, but we are seven miles away." He's scared, yet still, I hope that he won't give up.

"Gramps! Click on the National Weather site. They should give updates by the minute. Read them."

"Let's see, right here. This is the area of instability and wind shear leading to tornado formation conditions, right in the area we are headed into!"

"*Man!* Where are we pulling over to? I have *no visibility!*" Frank firmly plants his foot on the brake pedal. I hear his Blackberry ringing. The name "Mom" pops up. Damn! Just what we need.

"It's your mother."

"Don't answer." Frank clicks a button and Hope magically goes to voicemail.

The back of my shirt is saturated with sweat, and my heart is skipping beats. I read the computer screen aloud, "Weather service says winds are blowing at eighty mph. With thunderstorm clouds, there is low-level moisture, and this blast of cold temperature is the perfect storm. It lifts the moist air aloft, and we have a tornado."

"Enough. This was not our best decision! We need to find shelter fast!"

"Go ahead. Gun it, Frank. *Go!*"

Frank smashes down onto the gas pedal, and the RV shakes loudly. The entire vehicle feels like it will disintegrate. I am afraid to look up and spot that dreaded funnel shape. I don't know whether to fear a twister or the RV blowing to God only knows where. Frank bears down on the vibrating steering wheel.

"Grip it, Frank! Try and steer to the side of the road. There you go, son. You can do it."

"What the hell?"

Frank manages to navigate over to the roadside. It is a dark, lonely patch of highway, and we land with a boisterous "thump."

He grabs a flashlight and steps out into the wind, as it blows the map from the dashboard. Within seconds, I hear him cursing as he yells in disbelief, "Damn, flat tire! We should have pulled over," he yells up to me. "I know you are in a hurry—" The last of his sentence is lost in the screaming wind. Frank stomps up the steps and with all his strength pulls the door shut. Saying nothing, he takes some flares out of a drawer.

"Is it safe to go out and place those on the road, son? What if they just blow away?"

"I just have to do something!" He sounds near panic, shooting a look of impatience. It's obvious he's thinking, "Grandpa, I just don't trust your judgment anymore."

He is severely rattled, and I wonder if we will get out of this alive. I know I'm dying, but I never intended to go like this or to be taking Frank along.

"Call emergency services," I say as he climbs back inside. His hair, face, clothes, and shoes are all drenched, and he's shedding water down onto the floor, his seat, onto me. I convince Frank he must stay put. The winds are quieter, and an eerie calm is in the air. All I can see out the window through the sheets of rain is a yellow light all around.

Frank and I sit at the kitchen table and wait. He is silent, staring at his hands, with fear on his face, his jaw muscles tensing, teeth grinding. There is nothing to say, each of us in our own thoughts, wrapped in mutual dread. There are those moments in life which are truly unforgettable. Waiting, this feeling of limbo in the eye of a storm and in what's left of a future filled with uncertainty. Things are not working out as planned. In the ominous stillness, I take refuge in my most cherished memory.

I will never forget the look in my young wife's eyes as she held our daughter after birth. That moment in time, so innocent and righteous, stands out from every other. If I close my eyes, I can still hear the doctor announce, "It is a girl," as he lifts her up into the air. If on some level I have compared each moment to this one, they come back lacking that purity. They would need to, as perfection is so rare.

Tonight, a different moment takes second place in my failing memory banks that being I have jeopardized my grandson's safety with a single-minded attempt to reach Faith. The phrase, "self-will run rampant," comes to mind.

The sound of sirens catapults my attention back to the present. Frank pulls back the curtains, and there are familiar red and blue lights careening on top of the rescue car. Frank helps me up and leads me down the stairs where a rotund, bald-headed police officer takes control. He says, "You guys get in the back seat, quick."

Before I can say, "Thank the Lord," Frank and I are taken a couple miles down the road. The cop car pulls into what looks like a deserted gas station with an attached car garage. My legs are wobbly, and I am still short of breath.

The policeman takes my arm, and we are led to what is called in these parts a storm basement. The trap door pulled up from the ground, and we descend semi-dark stairs. This basement will be our refuge until the tornado safely passes.

They are calling this particular tornado a Gustnado. It is weak and usually short-lived, forecast more as a temporary dust whirl, what my father used to call small ones, dust devils. Quick, crafty, then out of our lives. The silly name sounds too trivial; the force of our storm was significant. I question their judgment in saying "small."

The Gustnado's destruction would control our lives over the next twenty hours and alter the course of my journey; but for now, we plop on old oil drums in the dark, listening to the wind trying to get inside.

Frank sits bent over, his head in his hands, not reacting when I reach out to pat his cold, wet shoulder, emotionally shaken, and I can't blame him.

Chapter 14

*Those who dive in the sea of affliction bring up rare
pearls.*

—Charles Spurgeon

Last Chance Shelter
Indianapolis, Indiana

With the door shut snugly, I try to doze on and off during our hours in the bowels of the storm basement. We hear the tornado roar over us around midnight, sounding as if it would tear open the door and suck us out into the twister. Is my fate to die by an enraged tornado?

The wind persists, but by 3:00 a.m., it no longer sounds as if it has murder on its mind. At daybreak, much calmer and quiet, the sheriff escorts us to the Last Chance shelter for safekeeping. Apparently, the tornado has "friends" hanging out, which will keep folks on alert for a while.

In a fog of exhaustion and disbelief, we arrive at the Indianapolis shelter. The instant I cross the threshold, I know I am in trouble. This stopover for those displaced by the tornado is chaotic and noisy and produces an interesting mix of fear and anger. It turns out, the tornado proved to be a higher category than the mere dust swirl originally predicted by our rescue squad. I told you so!

We soon learn that our shelter is housing the folks who lost their homes in the western portion of the community. A quick glance around shows a wide array of people, mostly still in their pajamas and robes. Others are waiting in a long line at the far corner of the auditorium to receive donated clothing which will replace soaked and torn nightclothes.

It is customary for the Red Cross to show up at shelters in any natural disaster to offer various help, from food and clothes to basic medical care. One of the RNs, in blue sweats and old gray sneakers, wears a name badge, "Fortitude." She turns and speaks quietly to a young man, apparently giving him directions and pointing at me. I hazard a guess at her age to be around mid-sixties, but I wouldn't tell that out loud.

"Hold on! Let me help you, sir. I can get a wheelchair!"

The young man in a green pin-striped tunic, representing medical personnel in training, turns on his heels to find the chair.

"Blast it, lad, I don't need a wheelchair!"

He pauses, confused. This old man is defying the nurse's orders and preventing him from impressing her with his speedy performance.

"It's only that I notice you are having a bit of trouble. Walking I mean. Wouldn't want to fall, would we?"

"*We* are not going to do any such thing. Toss my bag in that wheelchair."

The boy stands frozen and uncertain, as "Fortitude" marches over to join us. Frank suddenly appears from behind with the rest of our duffle carriers.

"Young man," she barks at me, barely making eye contact. "There are policies in place for this sort of thing. I do not want any accidents on my watch."

When someone calls any male over the age of fifty a young man, that's strike one in my book. I am not inclined to good manners at the moment but make the effort.

"I am feeling a bit tired. That's all. I have never used a wheelchair, and I'm not in the mood to start now. Lead me to one of your cots, and I will be happy as a clam. Thank you ever so much."

I flash my best smile at her and hope it helps. She nods briskly, having been given a way to dispose of me. She grabs my right arm, Frank takes the other, and with the boy in training placing a hand on my right hip from behind, we all walk toward the cots. It feels absolutely ridiculous.

"Hey! There are empty cots over here."

One of those young girl punkers with the bright orange, cropped haircut and flaunting a gold earring in one of her nostrils points us toward a row of empty cots.

"Need some help?" she asks. And that just about does it for this old geezer.

"*Drat!* Will you all please get it through your collective heads? I do not need anything but a cot, maybe a hot meal and then to get back on the road."

The young girl returns to her book.

Fortitude returns, pulling a blood pressure cuff out of the pocket of her sweats, and without asking, straps it onto my arm.

"It's 160/97 high, all right. Sir, do you take any medication for hypertension?"

"Yes, I do. I already know about this issue. Been living with it for years."

"I suggest a medical examination. There is a doctor scheduled to show up in an hour or so from the next town."

"I understand your concern, really all of you, but I am only here on my way to see my daughter. Frank, tell them I am fine. As soon as the roads clear, my grandson and I will be on our way."

Frank is fidgeting nervously, not making eye contact with me. I am relieved to hear the young punker intervene with her own issues.

"When can we split?" She demands of the nurse. "I mean, when the roads are cleared, need to scoot. My aunt decides to take off for her sister's last week, leaving me with an old farmhouse to care for. I want out of this boring, piddling town."

"Hard to tell, young lady, whenever the highway opens. Clean-up crews are hard at work. Might I suggest a hot lunch for you folks? All set up over there." She picks up her medical bag of toys, stuffs the blood pressure cuff inside, and marches off to torment another soul.

"Hi. My name is Frank. And this is my grandpa." Frank holds his hand out to welcome our adjacent bunkmate.

"Hey. I go by Josie, not that you care." Frank looks as if someone threw water in his face.

"Umm." He clears his throat. "Just want to know who we are crashing next to, that's all. No worries."

"It's cool. Been in better moods. My creepy boyfriend left. All because I wouldn't put out. Fighting every step of the way with these people in here too. I have a short fuse when someone shouts orders. Can't trust them."

"It's all good, Josie." Frank has a way of talking which puts a person at ease. When he wants to, that is.

Josie is a gorgeous girl, though a bit rough around the edges. She appears to be around seventeen years old, give or take a year. Her belligerent, arrogant tones I sense are merely a cover for a lost little girl.

Frank decides to go and pick up sandwiches from the "diner" set up in the corner. I would kill for a cup of coffee and stress the importance of my caffeine fix before he leaves.

"You want something to eat?" Frank asks Josie.

"Wouldn't eat this garbage. Have you seen the men serving the food?"

"Suit yourself."

I'm not in the mood for any drama and decide to lie down. After a few minutes, I awake to find that Frank has returned with food and coffee. Josie is sitting on her cot next to mine. Downright exhausted, there is a conversation going on; I hear yet don't hear. It is kind of like when you are too tired to care. You know there is something going on, but you are too numb to take anything in. They sit on their cots engaging in a sporadic chitchat between bites when a young man walks up.

"Wasn't that the most incredible tornado? And so late in the season." This twenty-something fellow with a fresh crew cut is staring down at Josie.

She folds her hands in her lap and barely nods. Frank, a bit more outgoing, shakes the visitor's hand.

87

"We missed the tornado, though barely when my grandpa and I were whisked into a nearby storm basement. Not without a bit of a scare first." Frank chuckles, and I feel him glance my way. Not in the mood for strangers. I just want to get back on the road. I am sorely tempted to head for the door and hitchhike to Maine, with or without Frank. I settle for rolling over on my cot and pretending to sleep.

"I'm Scott. Proud to be a storm chaser in these parts. You guys from around here?" Scott's eyes are only for Josie.

"I am from West Coast, California," Frank says; but Scott continues to stare at Josie, who finally decides to participate.

"I've seen you on the local channel, you are the guy who gets in that obnoxious steel vehicle and chases twisters."

I peek out from under the sheet to catch Scott beaming from his success in capturing her attention.

"I get such a rush chasing these storms, but this time? Got a late notice about the tornado, couldn't get off work before the highway patrol had shut down the roads. Storms being unpredictable, they err on the side of safety. Not much fun for storm chasers. Anyway, here I am. Storm vehicle never got out the gate."

"Yeah, very disappointed." Then he brandishes Josie a wide grin. "Until the next one, that is."

"Never a dull moment on chases, huh?" Frank has jumped back in. Josie's attention has returned to her lunch.

"You got that right. My degree is in meteorology. I report on weather at the station KSTV. But my adrenaline rush comes from tracking storms."

"Seems like you've got your life together, man. I mean, an interesting degree, job full of variety and a little excitement on the side." Frank sighs, shrugs his shoulders, and says, "Guess I am at what you would call, a crossroad in life. Well, in everything. Hard to sort it out."

"Oh, poor baby! With guys it's all about you," Josie interrupts. "You don't have this, you need to find that, need space to do, whatever."

Josie aggressively pulls her hoodie over her head, missing the annoyed look on Scott's face. Square in the middle of her left wrist is an obvious self-inflicted cut across the veins. Just from a quick glance, I'd say she did it about two weeks ago.

Now I am lying on this cot, stuck in this God-forsaken place, with people I don't want to know, and plain old worn out. Just listening to their mindless chatter makes me tired. When I think about standing up, my body cries out to stay put. I hate this feeling. Josie and I are both angry, but for different reasons.

Scott is split between self-absorbed chatter and his attraction to Josie. I vaguely remember my youth, eons ago, being just as insensitive. Scott continues, "You are right, Josie. We men certainly have our faults."

"It's just that, well, it's hard to trust a man who walks out on a six-year-old daughter. What kind of jerk does that?"

"What do you mean?" Frank asks.

"I mean what I said, fool. My father up and left my mother and me, with barely an explanation or a pot to piss in."

"He's a loser. Anyone who would leave you, Josie, is a loser." Scott says, trying to get into her good graces.

"Hard to count on people. Ever since that day, when I start to rely on someone, they are gone! It's like being stuck watching the same rerun over and over."

"Living like that must be a downer," Frank joins in.

I wonder if either of these young men can become more insipid or obvious.

"Oh, I've done okay for myself. I am a survivor." Josie rubs the fresh scar on her wrist and looks Frank in the eye. "My plan is to ditch this joint and start a new life somewhere else. I have heard California is the place to be. The sunshine state, right?"

I try to slowly sit up on the edge of the cot. My body cooperates up to a point, then I feel a creeping numbness in my right leg.

Fortitude has climbed up onto a wooden box, megaphone in hand, and is announcing that the roads are open. "But there will be an occasional tree limb down, so please be very careful out there. A warning, you will not find the familiar landscape. The Governor has already requested emergency aid, which means FEMA is on their way. Try to hang on and help each other. If you have nowhere else to go, come back here. We are not going anywhere."

Folks begin gathering their belongings and heading toward the exit.

I am left with only two choices. I can either stay put and ask for help with that blasted wheelchair or try to walk it myself. Embarrassed and in a very bad mood, I fear I cannot stay up on my feet. Scott starts packing up and turns toward Josie.

"Josie, I really enjoyed talking. If you ever want to hang out, stop by the station. Practically live there these days. That is, when I am not chasing storms. You could ride along during the next one if you'd like."

"No way, I am moving on. Not sure where, but I'll know when I get there."

Josie turns away from Scott, picking up her white macramé purse.

"Josie? You know, not all men will let you down," Scott says quietly.

"Right."

Scott shrugs, says his goodbyes, and is gone.

Frank and I are ready to go too. Just the idea of walking out and climbing into the RV feels like approaching Mount Everest.

"Come on, Frank. Let's split this joint. We have some ground to make up for." Frank is in another deep phone conversation. He looks around nervously, mumbles, "Gotta go," and hangs up.

Now I may be on my last legs, but I can still recognize when a girl is developing a crush on a boy. And Josie likes Frank. Now that Scott has left, she turns her eyes toward my grandson.

With no energy to concern myself with youth and its follies, I concentrate on placing one foot in front of the other with Frank holding my arm, heading toward the door. Then in a flash, I start to tumble forward. A loud, booming obscenity explodes out of my mouth as Josie appears out of nowhere to break my fall. Wouldn't you know it, everyone and their uncle come running. Out of the corner of my eye, I spot that rotund nurse barreling toward us with that damn blood pressure cuff. For her age and weight, that woman can move.

I look Josie in the eye and plead, "Get me out of here." This sainted girl jumps up, and before the medical entourage can attack, she approaches with the hated wheelchair.

"I'll take him to get help," she states firmly at the approaching group.

Trying to throw them off the scent, I acquiesce and drop gratefully into the wheelchair. I now view the wheelchair as my carriage to freedom. Frank shakes his head as Josie pushes me rapidly out toward our vehicle, through the nonstop rain. The RV delivered, after makeshift repairs; how anyone did that during a storm is impossible to imagine. Together, Josie and Frank help me up the steps into the RV, and I am back in my copilot seat.

"Frank, why don't we drop this young lady off at her home?"

Josie agrees, and the three of us head out of the Last Chance Shelter toward Josie's farmhouse.

Destruction is everywhere. There are remnants where once there were houses. We drive through the central portion of Indianapolis; buildings are collapsed, demolished into splinters and kindling. We see an occasional chair or ironing board left standing undamaged. There is no logic in this insane landscape.

"Turn down this road Frank," Josie directs.

We find ourselves farther out in the country.

"Oh God! The greenhouse bit the dust," Josie yells, "Incredible. This is like being in a dream."

"More like a horror film, I'd say." Frank is fed up. Who could blame him?

"Turn here," Josie almost whispers.

As we turn onto the roadway, there is this deep aura of loss and abandonment. It is as if God himself is deserting us. I glance out the right window and see people walking with torn, bloody clothing, their eyes searching for something, anything familiar. They look up at us as we pass slowly, the same question on all their faces, "Where do we go from here?"

"Off to the right is my aunt's house," Josie points over my shoulder.

"Crap! The farmhouse is gone. Been in the family since 1932. My God, the only thing still standing is a couple of trees. And that old hay rake.

"What I thought would survive is gone, all gone." Josie continues, "Funny how things end up, huh?" She turns her head away and wipes her nose on the back of her hand.

What am I doing in this awful situation, listening to this girl who has been abandoned by her father? And now Mother Nature has done her worst. Josie is alone with no place to lay her head.

"Looks like I am homeless," Josie says as she scans the scene. "Just drop me off over there by the willow tree. My mother planted that when I was born."

"Isn't there anywhere else we can take you?" Frank starts to turn the RV around.

"Hey, I am used to fending for myself," she says with determination.

"Frank, may I talk to you? Excuse us a minute, Josie, will you?"

Frank pulls over to the side of the road. Josie steps out and sits down under the tree. There are passersby stopping to gawk at the ruins, and I just want to get out of here.

"I have a thought, Frank. I am feeling more tired these days and worried about the toll all this driving is taking on you."

"Yeah?"

"Well, why don't we offer to take Josie along? She has nowhere to stay right now, what with losing her home and all. She is looking to move somewhere new and have an adventure."

"Oh, I don't know, Grandpa. Seems a bit out of nowhere to me. Why?"

"Why not? We can help her. She can help us."

"Win-win, huh?" Frank does not look too happy but agrees with my scheme.

He opens the door and goes down the steps and over to Josie. She is resting against the trunk of her mother's willow, coming up with a plan, I suppose. She has picked up a teddy bear from under the tree. "This isn't even mine," she says as Frank approaches.

"How would you like a ride to the East Coast? Gramps and I are heading there, and I could use some help driving." Her face turns forward, thinking for a minute, then bolts out a hearty, "Sure!"

She picks up her purse and the teddy bear and runs for the RV door, smiling as she leaps up the steps. "Thank you, Gramps. Thank you!" Frank brings up the rear, closing the door, still looking dubious.

Josie will be a much-needed companion to help on the last lap of this journey. God works in mysterious ways. Sometimes we are sent a helper, a support in the most unlikely package. This one comes with short, frizzy orange hair and a nose ring. What else could I need?

I remind myself not to judge by appearance nor circumstance that we all need to keep an open mind and open heart. If we ask in prayer for assistance, chances are good; we will be sent someone who can direct us where on our own we are afraid to go.

Chapter 15

When you can't look on the bright side, I will sit with you in the dark.

—Alice in Wonderland

Grandpa, Frank, and Josie
On the Road to Harrisburg, Pennsylvania

"Another hour and I'll turn the wheel over." Frank is relieved to share the driving with Josie, our new fellow road warrior, who happily agrees to help. He is no doubt tired of popping those NoDoz tablets.

Our itinerary heads toward the town of Harrisburg, Pennsylvania. This is roughly a ten-hour straight shot east, and I hope to God we don't have to stop for anything else. Every cell in my body screams for relief from frailty. I decide to sleep until we reach our next destination. Kicking off my penny loafers, I call out, "It's afternoon, young folks. I'm going to sleep!"

"Oh no, Gramps. Not until I whip you up some grub. Always sleep better on a full stomach. Now let's see what you bachelors have in stock."

Josie doesn't wait for an answer. In the blink of an eye out come flour, eggs, milk, cinnamon, and a frying pan. She begins whisking this marvelous mixture, which soon exudes a heavenly aroma.

"Any pancake syrup?" Josie asks.

"My daughter Hope set up this kitchen. Frank and I have hardly explored its contents. Feel free to check it out."

Josie finishes her kitchen magic, and we sit together and share a meal so simple, yet I am savoring every morsel. Some people just know how to cook, and I wonder how this young girl learned to create this five-star breakfast using only basic ingredients.

"Who taught you to cook? Your mother, I bet?" The pancakes melt in my mouth. The bacon is the perfect amount of crisp. Even the eggs have a wonderful flavor. This food feels so warm and luxurious. I remember my own dear mother by her kitchen stove. She brought safety into any darkness.

Josie interrupts my reverie. "My mom. Cook? Crap. Do you have that wrong."

"Um, it's just that you really seem to know your way around a kitchen. A mere assumption. By the way, I assume you to be eighteen already. Don't want to get pulled over for kidnapping." I chuckle, but the thought had crossed my mind.

"Yeah. Turned eighteen two days ago. You don't have to worry. There is no one looking for me."

"I overheard that your dad has been out of the picture?"

"Mom never talked about him. I think there was another woman involved, and I was pretty young, only six. Though I vaguely remember fights, nasty ones. What were the fights about? Don't know. Don't care."

"What about your mother? Did she raise you alone, or—?"

"Mom is cool. Well, of sorts. I mean she lives with her ups and downs."

I pop the last delicious crumbs of comfort into my mouth. Putting down my fork, I pick up my plate to drop in the sink on the way to bed. Josie however needs to continue, so I pause.

"With Mom, it's, how can I put this? She is either with you every step of the way, or you know you better get out of *her* way!"

"When did you start living on your own?"

"When my aunt left to chase a job. I grew up with mom, but there were times she dumped me, long, endless days staring out the window and watching for her car to drive up. You know the empty field we saw? That spot is where mom dropped me off when she was in one of her moods. Like everything else, the house is gone, too."

"That type of life must have been hard for a girl growing up."

"Not really," she turns her head away.

"It's just I imagine all that bouncing around, not knowing who to count on. In my generation, I was raised to believe stability was everything. And yet, I—" My voice trails off as I debate about how much to share.

"Here, I'll take those." Josie takes the dishes and continues to clean up. As an afterthought, she turns and looks me in the eye.

"You know what kind of awesome mom I have? Who has a mother that does this? On my sixteenth birthday, I told her I wanted to have the name of where I'm going to live someday tattooed across my lower belly, *CALIFORNIA!*"

"And she locks you in your bedroom, right?" I have doubts any sensible parent is going to put up with this idea.

"That's the point, Gramps. Mom took me to see this friend of hers, Willis. Okay, so he put me on his kitchen table and brought over a tray of the most terrifying, pointed instruments. I am wearing a bikini under my clothes and am prepared to go through with this."

"Never had a tattoo myself. Heard they are mighty painful, have made more than one grown man cry."

"I'll get to that. Now picture this. I am lying on the hard table. Willis was huge. I'd say six feet, eight inches easy. He towered over me even sitting down. He carefully lined up all his torture devices on an old but clean white linen towel. He stared down.

"He took my hand, turned my face to look at him, and said, 'Little Miss, a tattoo this big, this long, I have done them before. The tough men who have gone through this? I have watched every one of them cry, whimper, and beg to stop. You know what you are in for, right?'

"Now I had talked about this *CALIFORNIA!* tatt for months and was my major goal. I looked over at Mom, and she merely nodded, reassuring I can do this. She pulled her chair up to the other side of the kitchen table. 'I won't leave your side until it's over,' she said.

"Mom sat there for five full hours while Willis inked out the tatt. I only stopped him once to get up and walk around after he drew the words on my stomach. It tickled. Once the needle started, I toughed it out, ground down my teeth some. The pain was way more than I had expected. Mom never said a word, just held my hand the whole time. Now that I think about it, she didn't even go to the bathroom until it was over. And today? Look!" Josie pulls the front of her sweatpants down to show off in beautiful, flowery script *CALIFORNIA!* inked in bold reds, greens, and violet, glowing on her golden skin.

I sigh. This girl has real guts.

"Now it's your turn, Gramps. What is your shining moment? Up until now, that is," she says with an openly devilish smile.

We both let out a laugh. I have just been reminded by the sight of this lovely young woman's skin that I am not dead yet.

*****

All the silence and shame over Faith's mental illness were always mirrored in the expressions of family and friends. Even one of the medical professionals laid the curse of blame on my doorstep. This was back in the 1960s, and parents were often scrutinized for what surely must be their part in their child's illness. I decide to go ahead and share with Josie the moment which sent my life off in a different direction.

"Josie, I have a daughter, Faith, whom Frank and I are driving to see. I have not seen her for over forty years. There were moments, important moments, when I was at Faith's side, just as your mom was there for you." Josie pours another cup of coffee and sits close.

"Faith was barely fifteen, and my wife and I had spent several years taking her for medical testing, psychiatric assessments, professionals weighing in on our family, and medication trials. This particular day, the weather was cold, and my wife, Faith, and I waited in the office of Dr. Dittsmeyer, chief of pediatric psychiatry at the hospital. Funny, all these years and I still remember his name, Brandon Dittsmeyer. Crude, obnoxious fellow, I could sense him coming down the hallway. The air turned frigid when his type A personality entered the room. He breathed aggression and purpose. But he couldn't look you in the eye.

"Dr. Dittsmeyer had requested this meeting to announce his conclusions on Faith's case. Before sitting down, nervous energy caused his hands to fidget over the pile of papers containing Faith's report. I remember as he sat down, his arm slid the top sheet off toward the floor. I was sitting on the left side of the massive mahogany desk. As the paper floated slowly down to land, I grabbed it to hand back to him. I glanced at it, and time stood still."

Even today as I tell the story to Josie, my heart races. I slow down, reminding myself to breathe.

"Are you okay, Gramps? Take your time. We don't have to continue if you would rather not." Josie places her hand on mine. Yet, I need to finish.

"Clear as day, the scariest, life-altering words imaginable screamed out from that paper. I saw our future first, before my wife, before Faith, before the doctor could tell us. There it was, Faith's life reduced to one line, 'Final diagnosis: Paranoid Schizophrenia.'

"Now, Josie, back in those days, schizophrenia was a taboo subject in polite society. Medication was gruesome and either sucked the life out of you or resulted in cogwheel tremors which frightened people away. Media portrayed sufferers as having little hope for a normal life or victims of shock treatments which left you more vegetable than a person."

"I know about fear, Gramps. I have a friend, an awesome guy who lives with bipolar disorder. He met his girlfriend in a recovery group. She lives with bipolar also. Well, Christmas came around, and he decided to bring this girlfriend to dinner at his parent's house. His mother threw a fit and set her foot down, said the girlfriend's behavior is unpredictable and embarrassing. 'There will be out-of-town relatives, and who knows what they will think.' So my friend didn't show up. He had a breakdown instead of the holiday. The pitiful part was that his mother was relieved!"

"Wow, Josie, that's pathetic. People are so judgmental about what they can't understand. That is why I was so afraid for my Faith."

"Shame, we are surrounded by it."

"You see, Josie, the instant I saw the words 'paranoid schizophrenia' on the report with Faith's name on the same line, I got physically sick. I handed Dr. Dittsmeyer the paper and kept quiet about what I had seen. Inevitably, of course, the minutes ticked on, and Dittsmeyer got around to reporting the diagnosis out loud. The silence was deafening. Then I asked him, 'But you can fix it, right?'

"Dittsmeyer while averting my gaze, shakes his head. 'Well, there are some new drugs in clinical trials. We will try to get her into one of the studies.'

"My silence was interrupted by my dear wife's sniffles, which later that night became loud sobs as reality sank in. For once there was graceful silence from Faith's room."

"I know people who live with mental illness. Heck, my mother has a mental illness. I bet I have some sort of anxiety. We all have something to deal with. But, Gramps, I wouldn't be rigorously honest if I didn't tell you all of it."

My ears perked up. There are certain words that when heard tell people in the program that they are in the presence of another recovering alcoholic.

"What do you mean, Josie?"

"When I was a little kid, I lived in a world of alcoholics. Everyone in the family drank. There were drunk, noisy parties long after my bedtime. I got used to pulling a pillow over my head so I could sleep. The next morning there were full ashtrays, half-empty highball glasses, jackets left by visitors, and shoes tossed across the room. Sometimes there were broken plates, lamps, even furniture."

"Oh Lord, Josie, who took care of you? How did you manage, get fed, go to school?"

"Mostly I did it. Fortunately, we had a washing machine and clothesline so I could do my clothes. I would boil hot dogs, cook scrambled eggs, and make sandwiches. My mother did her best, but as I got older, more fell on me. Mom had periods of sobriety but gradually became less reliable. Once in a while, she would feel guilty and apologize, then go get another drink to ease her guilt.

"I had chores after every party: clean up, empty ashtrays, pick up broken glass, vacuum, and take out the trash. Took half a day to clean up after really bad parties. The mess even spread to the bathroom and bedrooms. Can't really describe how bad it was; you had to be there.

"I heard someone say more than once when the house was clean, 'Wow, the house looks great! We better throw a party before it gets messed up again.'"

"Do you drink, too, Josie?" I asked.

"I did. Oh boy, did I drink. It started with gulping down the stale leftovers from the party glasses the next morning. There would be a little booze left, and it made cleanup a lot mellower. I started drinking more and more. But had to give it up. Even smelling liquor became like walking barefoot through fire," she shook her head.

"How were you as such a youngster able to stop?"

"I was sixteen, and a boyfriend was going to a meeting and invited me to come. Hell, I figured it would be a kind of party. But we walked into this room in the basement of a church, with candles on tables forming a large rectangle. I just watched.

"Pretty soon there were fifteen people sitting around the table, and a guy began to read the principles of Alcoholics Anonymous. I started to get up and leave, but my friend grabbed my hand, smiled, and whispered, 'Please, trust me.' So I stayed, listened, and cried more than I had since I was a toddler. I kept going back, and reading, and realizing that there was a better way to live with myself and my family than I had been doing. So that's the rest of the story. You're in AA, too, aren't you?"

As she takes my hand and squeezes it, I feel she is one of those miracle gifts my higher power sends whenever I'm in trouble.

"I am, Josie. And I know it saved me. But I had to live with my actions. I ran away from the one I love. I didn't know what to do with my pain except to run. But it followed wherever I went. Deep down, I had to learn to live with leaving a piece of my heart behind. Being a father, I was supposed to protect. I worked and escaped and fought back the tears, but still, my daughter was in turmoil. Here I am, at my age, and the only thing keeping me going is that Faith needs to know. I must tell her I never forgot her and that I never forgave myself."

Drat! Here come the old familiar tears and knot in my stomach. I fight to hold them back, as usual. Men don't cry, right, Dad?

I look around the RV. How did I get *here*? Why can't I allow myself any mercy? I can't pretend anymore. I let my tears trickle, then increase to a gusher, as if every tear I stifled over the years has sat and waited for release. Josie tenderly slides her hand into mine.

"Come on, Gramps. Let's get you to that bed."

I hold this dear girl's hand and realize that despite all the abandonment in her own life, she is a survivor. I don't know what she typically does on a day-to-day basis, and I admit that at first, I had judged this book by its cover. But as she acts in service toward this failing old geezer, I no longer hear the angry tone of her voice. What she has shared of her childhood should have left her a basket case, yet she has a gentle strength and appreciates who she is. I can't help but believe her future is full of possibilities. I would give my life to believe that Faith has survived like Josie and has a life filled with potential, too.

Josie helps to lift my tired legs onto the mattress and pulls the blankets up over my shoulders. At last, in this cocoon of warmth and serenity, I can weep. This angel silently holds my hand as I cry until sleep sends me blessed oblivion.

Chapter 16

I've learned that home isn't a place, it's a feeling.
—Cecilia Ahern

Grandpa, Frank, and Josie
Harrisburg, Pennsylvania

Josie drives all night heading east, while Frank and I catch up on our sleep. I awaken and pull back the curtain to see the beautiful Susquehanna River. Josie steers our RV onto the bridge which will bring us directly into Harrisburg. Wonderful news, we make it to Pennsylvania in one piece.

The day has started out a humid seventy degrees at 8:00 a.m. with a forecast to top ninety-two. I hear there are occasional heat waves in these parts, and I expect September to be on the warm side. Oh well, it is what it is.

The greater Harrisburg area is the heart of fertile Pennsylvania Dutch Country. We pass a number of large, family-run farms, and there is a sense of history, continuity, and strength at every turn. As we come off the bridge and continue toward the town, I see the Pennsylvania State Capitol. Frank reports its impressive dome rises to a height of over two hundred and seventy feet. The building brings to mind the St. Peter's Basilica in Rome, after which it is modeled. Drat! Must everything conspire to remind me of St. Peter and my future trip to the pearly gates!

I stand up from bed slowly, testing the waters. My legs still feel weak and tired. Caffeine in massive amounts is in order. Frank is already up and dressed and from the looks of it, a bit rough around the collar.

"Good morning, kids. How about gramps treats to coffee? You know one of those fancy concoctions which take all day to order?"

Frank smiles, "Sounds like a plan. A town this size would have at least a couple bistros." Frank starts typing briskly into his blackberry, and presto, up pop the directions. We are only three blocks away from a Starbucks.

The three of us enter the corner coffee shop. The step through the door almost takes me down, and I remind myself to watch where I place my feet. Immediately, Josie's facial expression brightens as she sees a "Help Wanted" sign by the cash register. Frank and Josie order the same, a soy latte Frappuccino with a pump of caramel, double blended, whatever that is. Me? I just want a regular cup of coffee. It's harder to order that than the other stuff.

"Excuse me a minute, guys." Josie sets her Frappa-something down on the table. "I want to speak to the manager about that job posting."

The manager does talk to Josie and, after huddling together, filling out paperwork, and finally a handshake; they are done. Josie bounces back to our table showing off her pearly whites. This endearing vagabond of ours has accepted the job offered. How did she land a job this fast? I suppose it is the year she worked at her local coffee pub or the ServSafe certificate she just happened to have in her backpack.

Heck, truth-be-told it's because, beyond the bright orange pixie cut and pierced nose earring, even the nearly blind can see, she is a gem, a smart diamond in the rough.

After telling us she will be just fine and not to worry, Josie hugs us, thrilled to have a job already after the tornado destruction. Frank looks like he wouldn't mind sitting here for another week. But that nagging voice is calling me back on the road. I hold Josie's embrace a minute longer in my mind after she has turned to leave. Then, almost on cue, my shortness of breath is back bringing a cruel reminder time is running out.

"Come on, Frank. We need to get going." We climb back into the RV and return to our respective pilot and copilot seats. By my calculations, Maine is roughly eight hours northeast.

The private investigator I hired to find Faith discovered she resides in a quaint, coastal town in Southern Maine. I am thrilled to envision Faith living in such a beautiful spot. I wonder if she takes daily walks on the beach. Is there is a protected bird nesting ground nearby? As a little girl, Faith loved nature and enjoyed the humming-birds that searched for the flowers outside our garden window.

I fantasize Faith's life allows enjoyment of these simple plea-sures. I pray her illness allows more than a semblance of a peaceful life apart from hallucinations and delusions.

Was I a pivotal part of her suffering in this world? Did leaving her life form a negative cloud, or might it have turned out well? This is a possibility that had never occurred to me.

Frank fires up the engine as I start to read the local newspaper, The Patriot-News. "Let's see, where are the weather reports? Forecast of high seventies through the weekend. Weather is fine for Ogunquit. We are almost there. Full steam ahead." This rattling cough to my annoyance produces the most obnoxious-looking phlegm. Frank pretends not to stare, looking as if his blood pressure is escalating.

"Frank, we will stay on Highway 95 most of the way, then take the 495, which runs up into Ogunquit. I have Faith's phone number ready and will dial it up as we get into town. I am thinking a surprise swoop entrance might be the best."

"Uh, Grandpa?"

"Oh, I know what you are thinking. Maybe we should call ahead. Prepare Faith for our visit. I don't even know if she is able to live alone. Heck, is her mother still alive? You must think I am awful, not knowing these things."

"That's not it, Grandpa. I have been meaning to tell you—"

"Huh?"

"You need to know that I, that we—"

"Speak up already. Tell me what, dagnabbit!"

"I guess there is no other way to say it then straight up. Mom is worried sick about you, and—"

"And? And? For heaven's sake, spit it out!" I sense a storm brew-ing worse than our previous tornado.

"I have been trying to hold her back, and you know how hard that can be. But, Grandpa, do you think I don't notice the weakness in your leg? And breathing, I see how you struggle. Even your smile is lopsided. I don't know. I just—"

"I am not eighteen anymore, granted, and I am not in the healthiest shape. But I didn't realize you are this concerned."

"Mom is on her way!"

"What?"

"Mom. She is on an airplane, flying into the Harrisburg International Airport."

"Right now?"

"Yeah, she sure is. I am sorry I didn't warn you. It's just that I have been keeping an eye on you and—"

"Drat! That is *all* I need."

We drive in silence up to the entrance of the airport. Admittedly, my mind is torn a million different directions, and I resent this intrusion on my plans. I am so close to my destination, and though I fear my body may not make it, I want to give it a shot. Every night before I drift to sleep, I take out the picture of Faith which keeps her memory alive. As if I needed a picture to do that.

Chapter 17

*What am I to do at this moment? Certain choices are
not easy ones, and they come with a huge price tag.*
                    —Debra Marie DeLash

Grandpa, Frank, and Hope
Hershey Pennsylvania Medical Center

"**D**ad! Here I am!" Through the airport crowds outside the baggage entrance, Hope marches toward us carrying enough gear for an army. She is wearing a determined expression worthy of any warrior. I am proud to have such a strong daughter, but I wish she would take her resolve elsewhere.

"You don't travel lightly, do you, daughter?"

Frank has grabbed two pieces of her luggage, leaving Hope with her pink flowered duffle bag.

"What is in all this? Tell me you are not relocating to Harrisburg." I try to inject a little humor, but no one is taking the bait.

"Actually, Dad, these bags carry an assortment of medical equipment. If you will not bother to be monitored by a doctor, then I am bringing the clinic to you."

"I don't have time for all this. Don't you see? We are only hours from our destination. And I stand before you, still alive and kicking. Not much worse for the wear."

"Well, get this through your thick skull. I care about you and have flown all this way to take you home. Now let's get a quiet hotel room with a comfortable bed and hot meal. I can check your blood pressure and other vital signs."

I barely feel up to a confrontation, turning to Frank for backup. But I see from his expression that this may be futile. He is the one who called Hope in the first place. I agree to go back into the RV to discuss this over a late lunch and allow Hope to check my heart rate. In exchange, Hope agrees to forego the fancy hotel.

We scout out an RV site ten miles east, reaching the town of Hershey. A large chocolate factory is located there, and the fragrance is in the wind. No time for sightseeing, this is merely a courtesy stopover for Hope's sense of security and then back on the road.

Frank spends an hour to set up in our assigned spot. As we had not reserved the space ahead of time, we are stuck in the less desirable middle section. Experienced campers prefer to be around the edges where it is quieter. But I don't really care. Let's just get my checkup over with and convince my youngest daughter to get out of the way.

The minute I sit myself down at the kitchen table, while Hope prepares the medical gadgets, I discover a new problem. The Patriot-News I intended to read now looks like a blurry mess. As I hold up the page, the letters in each word shift sideways and in both directions. What the heck is this all about?

"Well, Dad, what is so interesting in the paper?"

"The paper? Same old stuff dear. You read one. You read them all." I set the paper down and roll up my shirt for the blood pressure cuff. Hope grimaces.

"Dad. Your pressure is up to 165/110. This is higher than usual, isn't it?"

She grabs my wrist and firmly presses her index and middle fingertips over my pulse. An eternity passes before Hope's somber declaration.

"Okay, Dad, enough is enough. Your heart rate is high at 120 beats a minute. Do you even know what normal is, for God's sake?"

"I know. I know. I am anything but normal these days. Haven't you ever heard the saying? Normal is merely a setting on the washing machine."

"Dad, this is not funny. Frank! Come over here. I need your help."

Frank finishes with hooking up the RV and appears irritated to be interrupted from his online blogging. He reluctantly turns.

I can't help but feel ganged up on as the walls close in from every direction. The last image in my mind is Frank running toward my chair and the hands on the clock moving sideways into oblivion.

*****

"Welcome back, sir. You gave us quite the scare." Opening my eyes, everything remains blurry except, that is, for the foolish grin on the young intern's face apparently assigned to my case. He looks young enough to be refused a driver's license.

"What is going on? Where are Frank and my daughter?"

"You are at the Hershey Pennsylvania Medical Center. Your daughter called an ambulance after you passed out. You woke up rather quickly on the way to the hospital, but, um, well, sir, you were sedated as you were rather belligerent with the EMTs."

"Young man. This is all a big misunderstanding. I actually feel a little better. You see, my daughter tends to overreact. Is that my test results you are waving in the air?"

"Yes. And I would like to call in your family while I go over them. We gave you a thorough work up."

The curtains pull back and in marches Hope and Frank. They enter as a team, and I can't help thinking that my control over this situation is going down the tubes. I am alone, with my adversarial family on the attack.

The young doctor reads the roster of ailments like a roll call of symptoms for several people. As expected, there is the lung capacity issue; the generalized weakness; high blood pressure; history of several TIAs, little pre-strokes I hardly notice; and a new one I didn't recognize. It is called wet macular degeneration with vision changes. I could barely get my thoughts together when Hope seems to read my mind.

"Doctor?"

"Johnston."

"Yes, Dr. Johnston. I have many questions, but this wet macular degeneration, that's a new one. Is this why Dad is having trouble seeing?"

Dr. Johnston spends ten minutes reciting medical mumbo jumbo, and soon my eyes are not the only ones in the room glazing over. Now I may not be the sharpest bulb in the chandelier, but any dummy can see I am in over my head. How will I ever convince Hope to let me continue this road journey now? If I weren't in such a condition, I wouldn't even need her agreement.

Frank grabs his mother's hand and appears to be at his own breaking point. I couldn't help notice those frequent drama-filled phone calls with his girlfriend have not lessened in intensity, and he is being torn in several directions. I feel as if I am holding everyone back from living their lives and have become a genuine pain in the neck.

Dr. Johnston and Hope agree there are two proper options to consider. One is to admit me to the hospital in Hershey where I will receive respiratory therapy and a series of intravenous clot-dissolving treatments. The second option is to have Hope escort me by plane directly home and to a local hospital for immediate follow-up care. They are leaving me out of the conversation.

I am, however, more concerned about my failing vision. I need to keep my eyesight if I am to accomplish my goal. I have begun writing a letter to dear Faith in the event I do not make it to her in time. I will need my eyesight for that.

I look at Hope and ask the question I am terrified to hear the answer to. But this is no time to beat around the bush.

"Am I going blind or what?"

Hope nervously tries to make sense out of the doctor's words, "Dad, this is how I understand it. Wet macular degeneration is caused by a leaking of small blood vessels in your eye. Well, the scan shows the vessels behind your eye are seeping blood into the retina. The result is what you are experiencing, problems seeing and focusing."

"Will this get better? Is it a matter of rest or what?"

"That is another issue," the doctor interrupts. "We need to call in a specialist, a retinal ophthalmologist. He can treat the area with injections of a medicine which closes off the leakage. You will need to be closely monitored."

"What are you saying? A shot in the eye? That is the cure? Oh no, not for me. Get my pants, Frank. We are out of here."

Frank, who has moved to the corner of the room, is sitting down, holding his face in his palms. Before I can say anything further, he jumps up and bolts out the door.

"Now what is wrong with *him*?" I ask.

Hope has followed Frank into the hallway, but there is nothing wrong with my hearing, and I am privy to all he is holding back. This is nothing short of an explosive tirade.

"What's wrong, son?" I hear the concern in my daughter's voice.

"Mom, I'm tired. That's all."

"Okay."

"Maybe a bit stressed. I am not sleeping well. Really miss my writing. It is the only outlet I have these days to deal with stress."

"What stress? Things are going great for you. Graduated at the top of your class, summer internship, and then landing that sought-after job as teen editor at the Goleta Daily. I thought you are happy."

"That is the problem. I don't feel any joy anymore. You know, it's funny, but I feel like Grandpa understands. My moods, all this, he gets it."

"I didn't sense all this is going on. Why didn't you tell me sooner?"

"About feeling depressed? It is just something no one talks about, wants to admit. You break your arm, and people swarm to sign your cast. But wake up in the morning and feel down, find it hard to get the energy to keep going? People I know, they would dart the other way. I get the impression some things are better left in silence."

"Frank, I don't know what to say. First, we need to talk Grandpa into coming back home. Everything else can be sorted out then."

"Yeah. Sure, Mom, whatever." He sounds discouraged and resigned.

I'm still sitting in the emergency room, feeling like the biggest jerk for putting my family through this. What right do I have to disrupt their entire lives based solely on a mistake I made so many years ago? Hope is strong, but Frank needs some guidance and a nudge in the right direction. I have put Frank under severe pressure. I should have just flown to Maine, not disrupted his life when he has his own problems. Where is my judgment?

Life is so unfair at times. I want to be around to help Frank understand there is a life beyond his depression. I fear the world we live in today will not give him that message.

What am I to do at this moment? Certain choices are not easy ones, and they come with a huge price tag.

Am I willing to pay the ultimate price in order to have the very thing I want the most? I am likely to die soon, whether I get to Maine, stay in Hershey, or get dragged back to Santa Barbara. My lifelong illusion of control has disappeared.

Chapter 18

Courage is not the absence of fear; it is the conquest of it.

—William Danforth

Grandfather
Hershey Pennsylvania Medical Center

1 have been sitting up since daybreak in what is fondly referred to among hospital staff as a "Geri chair." A Geri chair is a confounded contraption in which a nurse kicks a mysterious, hidden pedal to bring the chair upright. She places the reluctant, usually weak patient into it, then not too gently hurls you back into a reclining position, supposedly of therapeutic value. All the Geri chairs on the neurology floor are this disgusting, bright royal blue color. Believe me, there is nothing regal about this chair.

Mere hours away from Faith's house, what if I can't get there, then what if I'm too scared to talk to her, or what if I die in the middle of it all? If I am to believe the doctors, I'm on a speeding freight train toward the grim reaper, stuck in this infernal blue chair!

Where is that nurse, already? After repeatedly pressing the call button to no avail, I reach down, pull off one of my slippers, and proceed to throw it out the open door. Splat, I hear it land on the floor of the main hallway. The charge nurse, angry as all get out, explodes into my room.

"I saw your light, Mr. Goodwill. We are quite busy. Have you considered we have to prioritize the calls received at the nurse's station?"

She pulls down her bifocal glasses and allows them to dangle on the chain around her neck. I thought that to be a bit outdated, but I suppose no one advises Nurse Hatchet on fashion issues.

"This request of yours better be in the urgent category," she barks in my ear.

Why does everyone assume I am hard of hearing?

Summoning my last nerve, I decide to make that call to Faith this moment, before I change my mind. Might Faith want to drive over and visit me here in Hershey? We could be together, and then afterward, if Hope wants to take me home, I will have accomplished my purpose. My hands are shaking so hard I can barely unfold the piece of paper with Faith's phone number. The numbers are a bit faded. After all, they have waited patiently in my wallet for eight years.

"Well?" Nurse Hatchet is dripping impatience. She nervously taps the floor with her white Dr. Scholl's nursing shoe. Size twelve, no doubt.

"Bring me the phone, please. Right, yeah that's right, put it on the armrest. I have a hard time focusing on the numbers. Nurse—Hatchet?"

"I don't have all day, sir. You may call me Nurse H. It is quicker, and I prefer that to Hatchet."

"Sure. Okay. Nurse H, I am trying to call my daughter and can't seem to make out the last of these numbers. I wrote them down a while back, you see."

"What is this paper? Looks like it is left over from World War II." She laughs for the first time. I guess in everyone some sense of humor lurks, waiting to spill out on unsuspecting and severely ill patients. Sadism must be a required subject in nursing school.

"Just read the numbers." I press down and enter the first four digits and then stop, exasperated. "I can't see the last three numbers. I don't have all day either!"

Nurse Hatchet returns her outdated glasses atop her thin, pointed nose and reads the last three digits. "Nine, seven, two," she says, still too loudly.

"Are you *sure*?"

"Yes, I'm *sure*. Now I have other patients who need me for better reasons." She spins on her rubber heels and marches out the door.

Now it is up to me.

All we have is the present moment, right?

The phone rings once. Twice. Three times. I wait, and nothing. Faith is not at home. I'm on the verge of hanging up when, in the stillness of my disappointment, I hear it. There is this magical sound of the gruffest, most raspy voice I could imagine on this planet.

"Hello? Anyone there? Hello?" This is not the fragile, feminine sound of my Faith, or could it be? Did I get a wrong number?

With trouble breathing, and the phone receiver slippery in my hand from sweat, I nearly drop it. If I lose the call, I'll have to buzz helplessly for Nurse Hatchet. My heart races, and I fight not to pass out.

The room begins to swirl, and I think I'm imagining Nurse Hatchet beside me, grabbing the phone as it falls. She has reappeared to take charge, which is what she does. She makes things happen.

"*Hello*. Yes, I have a gentleman waiting to talk. Don't hang up, he is right here." I feel Nurse H. place the receiver against my ear and hold it in place. I take the deepest breath that I have ever taken. And then I exhale and feel the hope surge through my veins.

"Is this Faith Goodwill? Faith?" I ask, trying to sound normal.

"Who is this?" The voice blasts with annoyed intensity.

This raspy, earthy sound could only belong to my dear Faith. I am amazed at the possibilities of this life. Oh dear Lord, now what? There is the truth. Drat, there is always the truth.

"This is, uh, well, I am—"

"Tell her already. I've got other call lights to answer, don't you know?"

I suppose in some universe, cheerleaders come in all shapes and sizes, and Nurse H. is no exception. I imagine her in a cheerleader's short skirt, and then wonder why my mind is wandering off into such insanity at this most important moment.

I take another deep breath.

"This would be your father. John. I mean, this is John Goodwill."

"Who? You are not my father. My father is in the kitchen. What is this? I think you may have the wrong number."

I am not prepared for the sinking feeling in my gut and hope Nurse H. will not hurl platitudes my way. I imagine another man taking that special place in Faith's heart. Unwisely, I allow my mind to wander. I picture another man leading Faith in a dance to some sappy, romantic tune at her wedding. Perhaps this man carried Faith's cardboard boxes of clothing into her first college dorm room. The pain explodes in quiet tears I have practiced to suppress for eighty years.

"What is going on! Give me the phone. I will handle this." Nurse H. grabs the receiver with her sausage-shaped fingers.

"This is Nurse Hatchet at the Hershey Medical Center in Pennsylvania."

"No, No! Don't tell her I am in a hospital for God's sake!" I whisper with as much gumption as is left. The voice at the other end continues.

"I think you have the wrong number. I do not know a Faith Goodwill."

"But I have to find her," I whisper as she hands back the phone.

"I am trying to locate my daughter. Her name is Faith Goodwill. She would be sixty years old. Do you know her?"

"Sir, I am sorry, but I am a recent transplant to Maine. I don't know many people here and certainly not anyone by that name."

"But how will I find her?" I wail as Nurse H. hangs up the phone.

All I can think is that if I had the strength I would like to strangle the detective who *swore* to me that this was the correct phone number. I am helpless and angry.

No sooner does Nurse H. turn from the phone, when Hope enters with impeccable timing. I can see by the determined look on her face that she has embarked on a mission. I don't remember that invisible moment when Hope and I, daughter and father, reversed our roles. But clearly, Hope has now assumed the posture of boss and caregiver. I see no redeeming value in this getting older thing.

Hope is the only other child that I have. She grew up in the gorgeous Santa Barbara area and enjoyed the status of an only child. My overzealous work ethic created a comfortable lifestyle for Hope and her mother, private schools, summer vacations on Catalina Island, and a nose job to remedy inheriting my huge schnozzle. Hope is an organizer, a go-getter and is not used to taking no for an answer.

Nurse Hatchett pipes up loudly, "The doctor has scheduled your father for a series of tests. And we have set up treatment with our in-house retinal ophthalmologist for tomorrow. I need signed consent for the procedures. Are there any questions?" Nurse H. is valiantly hanging on to her own role of boss.

"Yes, I would like a detailed list of the tests, side effects, and the purpose, please." Hope jumps in with authority.

That Hope, what a gal. I have to admit I am proud of her no-nonsense approach and practical way of looking at life. I must have done something right. Nurse Hatchett leaves to retrieve the needed consent forms.

"Well, you told her, daughter." I chuckle a bit. It is necessary to hide my disappointment from Hope about not finding Faith. Hope doesn't appear to be comfortable in discussing this sensitive issue. I know she got the denial and avoidance tendencies from dear old Dad.

I decided to draw a line in the sand concerning these darn medical tests.

"You do know I have no intention to go through those barbaric shots in the eye. And those cardiac stents they talk about, not in the game plan either."

"Dad, listen to yourself. You're not making sense. The doctors have the ability to help you, to make a difference in not just the quality of your life but to help you live longer." Hope reaches into her purse and pulls out two long envelopes.

"What have you got there?" Stupid question, but I need to buy a little time.

"I have two airplane tickets, for you and me, a first-class trip back home. Frank says he will drive the RV back to Santa Barbara. You can get the best medical doctors in familiar, comfortable surroundings. Wouldn't you rather be in your own furry robe with a hot toddy by the fireplace?" I cannot look at her, too much emotion.

I whisper, "I am awfully tired. This whole trip. Well, things just didn't work out as I had planned." I'm amazed at how tiring this conversation has been, and I have nothing left to fight with.

"Dad, I recognize this is hard. Choices you made so long ago, is it really healthy at this point to be dredging it all up?"

"I don't know anymore."

"Come home. You have taken care of me all my life. Now, I want to take care of you."

Exhausted, I nod and reach over to gently pat Hope's hand.

She says, "All right, then. Let me get busy and make arrangements to have you transferred to Cottage Hospital. We'll leave in the morning. The sooner you are back and settled, the better. I will check with Nurse Hatchet about traveling with your oxygen tank and anything else you need." Hope jumps up at a dizzying speed. With her exits the last vestige of energy in the room.

I don't know what else to say or do. Faith's number is not the right one, and she is not listed in the phone book. Frank even looked her up on the Internet and Facebook, with no success.

I am a coward, afraid to face the needles and tubes which these doctors propose, terrified to venture out when I can no longer trust this old body. Every morning I wake up, I never know where my pain will be or whether I can hide the blurriness in my eyes, weakness in my legs, and the effort it takes to breathe. I can no longer avoid reality when I see it reflected back in the faces of those around me.

The last of my mental and physical energy swirls down the toilet as I realize that this is how the story of my life will end, with a colossal effort signifying nothing.

My father, who used to spend Saturday nights at the downtown card room playing poker, had this saying: "Son, a real man plays the best hand he is dealt, but when something is not in the cards, it is time to fold. No tears. You play your hand, then put your cards down and walk away."

Maybe father was right all along. It is time to pack my bags and return home.

Chapter 19

I said to the man who stood at the gate of the year, "Give me light that I may tread safely into the unknown." And he replied, "Go out into the darkness and put your hand into the hand of God. That shall be better for you than light and safer than a known way."

—M. Louise Haskins, *The Desert*

Grandfather
Hershey Pennsylvania Medical Center

"**G**ramps, is this the last of it?" Frank asks.

"Sure, son. Yep," I sigh.

"I don't mean any disrespect, but you don't look so well. I know it's hard to make this decision. I mean to come back home. But something in your eyes is missing. You are different."

"It is the light, Frank. My inner light."

Nurse Hatchet, who is quietly organizing my necessary paperwork in the corner of the room, approaches Frank. She hands him a folder with instructions for the doctors in Santa Barbara. She cannot keep her thoughts to herself any longer.

"You know, I have been a nurse for fifty years. In all that time I hardly took a vacation. You might say I love my work, and I do." She looks over at me.

"Probably your grandpa is the same way. They call us workaholics."

"Geez, you never thought of retiring?" Frank asks.

"Not yet. Guess I don't know what I will retire to. My life is within these hospital walls. Never married, and never had my own children."

"I suppose you will one day. I mean retire. And I am sure your patients will miss you."

Frank is trying to be polite but keeps looking my direction to swoop in and rescue him. I slowly stand up from the Geri chair and shuffle toward the closet to grab my sweater. My vision remains blurry, and I will feel relieved to settle into the safety of my home environment.

"You know," Nurse Hatchet continues, "my theory is all the work, all our actions to keep things moving, changing, are based on a belief we can control what happens in our life. We want to remain at the helm of the ship. And we end up running faster than the speed of our feelings. Some of us spend our entire lives running, yet never get to where we want to be. Won't understand it is out of our control anyway. Don't want to believe it. Until that is, one day reality stares us directly in the eye. The day we realize we will not live forever."

I feel irritated at this intrusion of philosophy by this grumpy, bigger-than-life nurse I just met.

"Mr. Goodwill?" Nurse H. glances at the bags, packed up and ready to go.

"Where do you want to be?"

"I want to be out of here, and not have to deal with this turmoil anymore. I don't know. Maybe I take it right along with me." She just won't stop talking!

"Sir, a person holds stuff in for a lifetime. Then at some point, we want a chance to do it all over again. We want to make things right for the ones we love. Yet we all reach the point when we start pulling away from the world. It is a normal part of aging. And what happens? We become like children again, only for most of us our childhood may not have been the ideal experience. We get to a crossroads. We can give our dreams one final push. And then, we know deep inside we are finished."

"Yeah sounds good and all. Maybe it belongs on a greeting card."

I stop and give Nurse H. a glance. "Damn it all, can a tiger really change his stripes in the last hour of the game?"

Frank is pacing and clearly is ready to exit this conversation.

"Come on, Grandpa. Looks like you're ready. Mom is waiting in the car."

Nurse H. pushes a wheelchair my direction.

"Hospital policy is I need to escort you to the car safely. Then, you are on your own."

Nurse H. pushes me down the long corridor, into the elevator, while Frank goes ahead to find Hope in the parking lot. Nurse H. and I are now approaching the ophthalmology department on the way toward the side exit doors. We reach the double doors which are the end of the line. Nurse H. is surprisingly quiet.

I need to see my Faith one last time, and I don't even know where she is! Drat, and Hope is waiting and plans to return our lives to the only normalcy she knows. I break the silence.

"I am going blind, and the only option is a barbaric ritual of plunging a needle into my eyeball? How is that for choices?"

Nurse H. halts the chair and stomps around to face me directly. She bends down to eye level. She is exasperated, I can tell. I am not the prize pupil she normally sees, no doubt.

She stammers, "What is the one thing in this world that you want more than anything else? The fact is, Mr. Goodwill, in this life for the things we want the very most, we may have to pay a big price. Are you willing to pay that price to achieve your deepest desire?"

I look up at her and say, "Wait a minute."

For close to five minutes, her words simmer like stew while she stands silently. Finally, I reach the boiling point and yell out, "Turn this damn thing around and wheel me into that door over there! The one marked Eye Clinic. Don't just stand there with your mouth open. I may change my mind."

Nurse Hatchett smiles and says, "No, you won't. No, I don't believe that you will."

Chapter 20

If you are afraid of the thorn, you truly don't deserve the rose.

—Melody Lee

Grandfather
Eye Clinic
Hershey Pennsylvania Medical Center

"Okay, Mr. Goodwill. This will be a short procedure," the eye doctor mutters quietly.

"Just get on with it. I need to be able to see, damn it."

"Let's calm down, shall we? Take some deep breaths, and we will get started, but not until then."

"Oh, there you are, Grandpa! Mom and I have been looking for you all over this hospital."

"Frank. Pull that curtain shut! And make sure your mother comes nowhere near this cubicle. I am getting the shot to restore my vision, and I am getting it now. If you can't handle it, wait outside the door." The doctor turns to Frank.

"Son, it really is not that bad. It sounds far worse than it actually is. Sit down over there and talk to your grandfather." He points to a chair in the corner. Frank sits down.

"All right, Mr. Goodwill, I need you to look down and keep looking down. Focus on a certain spot. Good, hold that." The doctor lifts up my eyelid, wham, bam, goes the needle to numb the eyeball. This gives me the major willies, but I survive the intrusive pinprick.

"Now, count to five hundred. This is how long it takes for the numbing medicine to work."

I focus on counting, and then right at two hundred and fifty, Frank interrupts, "What is this about, Grandpa? I thought you were going back to Santa Barbara with mom."

"I certainly am not. I changed my mind, that is, if I can find someone to drive me?"

I muster up the most charming smile and offer it to my grandson. At that moment, the eye doctor returns to his stool by my head and whisks out the hypodermic needle. I don't really know if it was the sight of the needle going toward his grandfather's eyeball or divine intervention, but as the needle pricks my retina, Frank cries out, "What the hell, how in the world do you expect me to say no?"

Moments earlier, I was convinced I didn't have the nerve to endure this barbaric medical treatment, and now the doctor is done. He tapes a bandage over my eye with instructions to keep it in place for several hours.

"All right, Gramps, now the moment of truth. *Mother.*"

Nurse Hatchett reenters the cubicle and once again begins to push me toward the exit. This time, I have Frank in tow and on board to continue this voyage. I tell him I cannot promise anything other than I am here now, my situation is precarious at best, and I will give this the best chance I have left. Come hell or high water, I will reach my Faith, or die in trying.

Chapter 21

Genuine feelings cannot be produced nor can they be eradicated. We can only repress them, delude ourselves, and deceive our bodies. The body sticks to the facts.

—Alice Miller

Grandfather and Frank on the road toward Ogunquit, Maine

Frank finishes loading up my walker with attached seat and bag of new medications. My exit scene with Hope outside the eye clinic was intense; Hope thought she had won the war, and I expected fireworks, and yes there were indeed. I have to pray that someday she will forgive an old fool for following his heart.

"Ready to get going, Grandpa? Let's run for it." He keeps looking over his shoulder, waiting for us to get caught. Frank speeds down the corridor and out the automatic door, which is barely opening in time with the help of my feet.

"Maine or Bust!" I yell approaching the RV.

Frank has his Blackberry out and says, "We should reach Ogunquit by 9:00 p.m."

I head back to my bunk and sit on the side of the bed, slowly removing the bandage from my eye. You have got to love modern medical science. The injection of Avastin works wonders. The blurry vision is already getting better, but I am not sure how long this reprieve will last.

"Frank? Bring me that Blackberry contraption. I need to pull up the Internet. I know Faith lives in Ogunquit but need to find the right phone number." I pull out the folded piece of paper with the numbers we tried the other day and hand it to Frank.

"Here, these are what the private investigator wrote down. There, area code 207-561-9972. That got me nowhere. If I could give that man a piece of my—"

"Grandpa!" Frank interrupts, sporting that impish grin he saves for special occasions. "Look at the first three numbers following the area code."

"Yeah, I did. I dialed those three numbers, 561, and Nurse H. dialed the rest."

"It's just that, this number one looks an awful lot like a seven. Is there any way you could have mistaken it?"

"Let me see. Drat! I see it is five, six, one, could be a seven, I guess."

"Let's try it again. I'm gonna punch in a seven just for the hell of it."

My heart skips a beat with every number Frank pushes on his keyboard. There is an answer on the first ring. This time the voice is serious, low in tone, with an eerie calmness I have waited forever to hear. This voice, my God, this is the voice of my Faith. I grab the phone as Frank stares. I see he understands. Isn't eyesight wonderful?

"Faith?"

"You have reached the residence of Faith Goodwill. I am out and about trying to change the world. I am certain if you have reached this number, I will want to talk to you. So, friends, at the sound of the beep, leave your name and number, and I will call. Shalom."

"Uh (a cough, cough), yeah, this is John Goodwill. I happen to be traveling through your area and was wondering if I can see you. I know it has been a long time. My number is (805) 986-5532. Answer me, Faith, when you have a chance." I hand back Frank's phone.

"She is not at home."

"You know, Grandpa, just a thought, but maybe you should have sounded a little more anxious about meeting her. If I were to get that message, it doesn't sound like you are in any rush."

"I don't know, Frank. The words just fell out of my mouth. Maybe I don't want Faith to know how sick I am. I don't want her to answer out of any sense of duty."

"Got it, well, whatever you think. So co-captain, what is your next plan?"

"Let's get this baby to Ogunquit and check into the RV park. Hopefully, by then, I will have heard back from Faith. Maybe tonight will be the night we go to Faith's house. In the meantime, I am putting these bones back into bed. I hear it calling my name."

"Okay. I'll wake you when we get there."

I need to see this through. I do not want to leave this world unsettled, realizing my anxiety must be calm if I am to survive long enough.

The word, "failure," spoken from my own father's lips echoes in my mind. Why did I choose to listen to his criticism over my own child's needs? If I had not believed those judgmental words, everything might have turned out differently.

My life, if I am to be honest, has been an exercise in futility as I tried to make my relationship with my father turn out differently. The man has been dead for years. Yet I have continued to mindlessly believe the prejudiced thinking of untold generations in my family. At what point in our shared bloodline did the harshness begin?

Why did I seek out relationships with people who saw the world as he did?

I've lost the urge to sleep, and I need action. I grab the notebook, brand new and full of empty, lined yellow paper. This may be the only connection left with my phantom daughter, the one who exists only in a memory and on a voicemail greeting.

I am not a writer, nor am I creative or tuned in to where feelings are concerned. How will I find the words to make a difference to the fifteen-year-old girl I left behind? Will she, at sixty, even be willing to read it? There is no time for anything but painful, gut-level honesty.

I will start this letter and pray to God that Faith has not lived her life mentally trying to recreate her lost relationship with me.

*****

125

The sun is setting. I know Frank is battling his own moods, trying to put aside his growing depression and get me to Faith's house. This letter will be my insurance that if I fail to see Faith, at least she may have her answers. I take one more glance at what I have written so far:

My Beloved Faith,

Frank your nephew, and I drove your half-sister Hope's RV, cross county to find you and if reading this letter, I did not make it in time. We traveled day and night and though my words are late, please listen to what I say. I have spent a lifetime re-living the day I drove to California leaving you and your mother behind. You deserve the truth about why I ran and my understanding of why I never returned.

My most cherished moment was when a little piece of heaven, our Faith was born. Back in the 1950s, fathers were not allowed in hospital delivery rooms. I was directed to wait at the end of a long corridor, downing cold, black coffee. I could hear my Sarah screaming and she sounded so scared. My emotions took over. I dashed down the hall, around the corner, ignoring the firm imperatives of medical folks, and burst through the doorway. As I focused my eyes on the bright overhead light, the doctor grabbed your squirming body, held you up in the air, and yelled, "It's a girl!" Every other moment pales in comparison to that precious snapshot in time.

I do not understand what happened in your brain chemistry that caused such turmoil in your teenage years. Your pain became mine and I tried to run away from it, not realizing the choice I made, thinking temporary, would become per-

manent. I could never find rest on any other path
but the one back home to my Faith ...

I tuck the beginnings of this letter underneath the mattress, so Frank does not see it yet.

Still no word from Faith, I take refuge for the night as my grandson hauls this RV down the dark road. Maybe Frank is right, and I need to share my sense of urgency with Faith. My body is not cooperating physically and screams with emotion, as I prepare my spirit to face the next days. As the moments tick on, there will be no running away.

Chapter 22

Like a wildflower she spent her days, allowing her-self to grow, not many knew of her struggle, but eventually all knew of her light.

—Nikki Rowe

Faith
At Home
Ogunquit, Maine

I love Saturday mornings and awaken grateful for another day of sobriety. Working in an art gallery on Perkins Cove offers a chance to chase my creative dreams, all within sight and sound of the sea. I imagine myself as one of the famous artists, elegant and free.

With no alarm clock, I slept until 10:00 a.m., and time stretches ahead with unlimited possibilities. I put on my favorite calf-length skirt made from hemp and cotton. Eco-friendly, growing hemp requires no pesticides and little water. It renews itself with every growth cycle. I believe it is important to leave this earth better for the next generation. This is the driving force behind all that I try to do. For whatever reason that my Creator decreed that my life is to be spent this way, I obey and follow the directive. That sounds like a phony goody-goody tree hugger, but I do it because it's fun and feeds my soul.

After buckling my Clark sandals and hastily finishing a waist-long braid, I am ready for Joseph to arrive. At sixty years young, I began dating Joseph last winter. Friends on and off for several years now, Joseph and I met in our church ensemble. Self-taught, I play the flute, and Joseph plays the oboe.

On our first picnic, we talked for hours. We discussed our appreciation for classical music and critiqued the various concerts we had attended. As fate would have it, we both commit to hosting a booth at the annual Homeless Community Kitchen Fundraising Festival. Held in Raleigh, North Carolina, every September, the Loving1Home organization invites artists, writers, and musicians to participate and help raise money for their "Feed the Homeless" pantry. Joseph and I are on the board at Loving1Home and will leave tomorrow for our yearly trip.

On the way to answer the doorbell, I pass the phone and notice there is a blinking message on the recorder. I push Play. It is the faint voice of an elderly gentleman. He sounds nervous, slightly out of breath, as if he had been running a race. Goosebumps rise on my arms. Is this really happening?

Incomprehensible, emotional confusion seems to be the message, punctuated by the shocking words, "This is John Goodwill."

I really don't want to deal with this. Why is he calling me, and what does he want?

At fifteen, trapped in a mind which betrayed me at every turn, I trusted no one. Who would stand by my side as I walked through the gates of hell? Surely not the man leaving this message. I am jolted back to the present with loud thumping sounds at the door.

"Faith! Faith! Are you in there? It's Joseph."

"Sorry, I'm coming."

The question of my father had never come up. How much am I willing to reveal to my boyfriend? What do I want to explain about events, actions, and their consequences that happened so long ago? Will there be a cost if I do share this? In my life, my father has been a nonentity since that terrible day over forty years ago at the Boston Psychiatric Hospital.

It was a chilly October morning, and the leaves were turning gorgeous shades of reds, oranges, and yellow. The colors were more real to me than anything else. I wanted to follow them, spinning up into the sky and over the roofs to anywhere the wind would take us.

I saw one that had green, orange, and burgundy all in the same leaf. I determined that I would be that leaf someday.

My fantasy was interrupted by my mother's voice calling me back to reality. Was her world more real than me flying with the wind as a tricolored leaf? One of those questions is what other people always have an answer for. Back then, I didn't even know how to define the word "real." As I walked out the institutional doors into what would be a lifetime of the recovery process, it was only mother who waited by the car. My father was already gone.

The sky had become overcast, with no shadows on the streets, as if my father took the sun with him, on that day of abandonment. In some ways, I have lived in denial since. The darkness of the day cast far-reaching clouds which have taken many years to allow the sun back in. I suppose it was there, the sunlight, but I couldn't see it.

I feel the anger welling up in my chest.

"What on earth does he want? Why does he contact me now?"

Joseph stands staring, waiting for some sort of explanation to why I am visibly shaken. I try to return his look which is a mixture of kindness and puzzlement. But this phone message has rocked me to the core, and I find no words.

"Faith, you look terrible, girl. Have you seen a ghost?"

"In a way I have, heard from one at least. I just received a message from my father. Apparently, he is passing through town and wants to stop by. The nerve, after all these years. What is he looking for? I have nothing to offer him. Nothing!"

"Your father? You have never spoken about him, and I just assumed he was—"

"He does not exist to me, Joseph. He walked out of mother's and my life after I received my diagnosis. Didn't leave an explanation or anything. I don't think he knew where he would end up. He told mother he was driving to California, saying he "always liked the weather out there." Sunny California. It's strange; I was just there last month, my visit to the LA County Jail for the article on lack of treatment for mentally ill. How ironic, I thought, to be in the vicinity of my own father and not know how to contact him.

Doubt I would have, even if I had known how. Now, out of the blue, he calls. Why now?"

"You and your mother never heard from him? What kind of creep does that to his family?" Joseph is pacing now, something he only does when he is about to explode.

"I used to try and make sense of it. Then one day, I realized I had stopped thinking about him. I'm sure my teenage behaviors were not only hard on mother and me but my father as well. I even cut some slack knowing he and mother had become parents far too early, barely out of their teens."

"You are far too generous, Faith."

"Things at home weren't always bad. When my psyche began to splinter into strange pieces of moodiness, anger, and withdrawal, a constant tiredness ate me up. I became obsessed with pulling my hair out. Father would try to bribe me by promising to buy special outfits for each day I kept my hands down. I don't think my parents recognized this as a medical symptom that needed attention.

"A lot about mental illness was not understood in those days. At first, I was called manic–depressive, but later my parents received a formal diagnosis of paranoid schizophrenia. Even my diagnosis proved confusing. All that mattered is our family life changed dramatically.

"Father began working late hours and rarely spoke when at home. Mother would cry alone in her room. At the time I didn't realize this was their response to my mental illness. I just thought they no longer loved me. I thought everything that happened was my fault, yet I couldn't make it stop.

"I began to turn to alcohol as a solution to the pain. I would put down a third pint of gin for breakfast on the way to school, and another one on the way home. I was drunk all the time but getting better at hiding it. It was the first thing I was good at, fooling everybody with my secret.

"I started hearing a voice telling me to do stuff. It would say my name 'Faith.' Had the feeling that it was a good thing but was afraid to believe it. No one else could hear it. It seemed to be telling me to do things that were good for me or someone else. I tried to tell mother, but she told me not to talk about it. I told my father one morning on the way to school, and he got really quiet. I thought he was mad and started to apologize when he pulled the car over to the side of the road.

"My father told me, 'I had a grandmother who heard a voice like that, Faith. People thought she was nuts. She was adopted from a home for unwed mothers. The story has been whispered in my family for generations. It seems that her mother had been raped and got pregnant. Her family sent her to a home in Massachusetts to have the baby, and she was adopted at birth. They were pretty good at cover-ups in those days. The only reason the story has survived is because she was related to Dorothea Dix, who became famous for mental health and prison reform. I never knew how much of it was true, but I remember my grandmother would talk of her spiritual dreams, and if she said, "Don't leave the house today," we believed her and stayed inside. I have told your mother about this history, but it seems to give her the creeps. So let's have it be our secret, okay? If you want to know any more, just ask when your mom isn't around.'"

Faith continues to tell Joseph, "I kept the secret for him and didn't ask anymore. But I would wonder if the voice I heard had anything to do with my grandmother's. I was afraid that I was causing myself to be sick, just by thinking about it.

"I believed people were constantly staring or talking about me. Whenever I was at home, I shut all the drapes tightly. My mother's facial expression in those days was one of devastation. Her sweet daughter was turning into a complete stranger."

Joseph broke into my trip down memory lane.

"This phone message, are you going to answer it? Are you going to call him back?" Joseph scoots his chair next to mine and slips a hand over my shoulder. "Faith, your sobriety and all, you have fought so hard for so long in your recovery, and well—"

"I know, Joseph. His coming to visit after all these years could be a trigger to relapse."

"Faith, I know how hard you have worked on this presentation to the Loving1Home board. It is the day after tomorrow. With your father's call, what do you want to do?"

"Go out and get the packet in the back seat of the car, would you? We need to go over the bullet points. I'll deal with my father later."

Joseph returns with an armful of reports and diaries which describe living conditions of the mentally ill in the Los Angeles County Jail. I spent an entire week visiting inmates and talking to their families and guards. I even attended the supervisors' meeting and spoke as an advocate with proposed solutions to the deplorable situation these folks find themselves in. The subject hits deep, as the closest person in my life today, Joseph, used to live repeatedly from jail to the streets and back again. And I know, "There but for the grace of God," I would be in the same desperate life.

"How am I going to take this cold data, Joseph, and bring it to life? I could not believe the jail houses over three thousand souls diagnosed with mental illness and accused of a crime."

"Yeah, when I cycled in and out of jail back in the 80s, you would see the same offenders. Many there for drug possession and minor offenses for which the underlying cause is mental illness. When they ran out of space, the folks with mental illness are housed with the general population. Victimized by their illness, by criminals, and finally failed by society. Terrible."

"As bad as that is, Joseph, it cannot be worse than the conditions I saw in the LA Twin Towers. Remember that dreadful, ancient building? On the top floor, the sickest men stand in locked single cells of a dorm-style bloc, staring into space, banging on walls or howling. On another floor, cells are filled to capacity, and bunks are squeezed into the common dining area. The bunks are two beds high, sometimes three."

"Deplorable, I know, dear. That jail has been called the nation's largest mental hospital. Jails and prisons are the mental hospitals of our times, and society has become used to it. The atrocity is this whole system of so-called care."

"Joseph, going in and out of the jail, I noticed sheriffs and staff on a first-name basis with many. It's a revolving door of pain and helplessness. I walked down the hall, where a fifty-three-year-old inmate squatted and spoke through a small opening in a locked door, diagnosed with paranoid schizophrenia as a young man. I asked how many times he's been in jail since then. 'About sixteen,' he guessed. He's been locked up close to twenty-seven years. Still there today, I'd imagine. While I spoke to him, another middle-aged man kept gesturing through a window that he wanted to talk, too. I am haunted by these images and the horror of why in the year 2013 we are still locking up the mentally ill."

"Agreed, dear." Joseph nods, almost in tears. "These poor people are serving time for the crime of being afflicted. Is this the 1800s or what? Bedlam days are here again."

I can only pray that our lobbying efforts will do some good.

Joseph and I believe in the ripple effect that if enough people speak out maybe one day the horrors of this dreaded diagnosis will change. I believe the people who are living with mental illness are the "forgotten." People forget or shun that which they cannot understand or change. I work every spare moment of my days to make a difference for this generation and the one which will follow. I am alive, living a normal life because there were people who helped me. I couldn't live with myself if I stopped trying.

The phone rings.

Joseph had left moments ago with plans to pick me up bright and early tomorrow. I notice he left his report for the board meeting on the kitchen table. I pick up the receiver.

"Hello, Joseph?" Silence. I hear a man cough so deep it is startling in its clear announcement of illness.

"Hello? Is anyone there?"

"Faith. Is this Faith Goodwill?"

"Yes, sir." Another long silence as I am about ready to hang up. One of those telemarketers, I suppose.

"This is John, your father."

Now I like to think I am fairly well adjusted and in control of things; after all, I have spent the past forty-five years working on my problems. But hearing the sound of my father's voice suddenly brings memories crystal clear as if on a big screen TV in my mind. In the blink of an eye, painful old feelings resurface, and I feel fifteen all over again. I am that rejected young girl exiting the psychiatric hospital, climbing into the car with only mother to deal with our unforeseen future. The old blanket of abandonment threatens to smother me, and I'm having trouble breathing. My voice is shaking.

"Why on earth are you calling me? What do you expect me to say when out of the blue you reappear?"

"I guess, I hope you may agree to see me. We have so much to talk about."

"Frankly, I don't see it that way. And tomorrow I am leaving for a very important trip."

"I just thought, maybe, you will allow a quick visit. Will only stay ten minutes. I know you must be busy, and I am merely passing through town."

"I'm sorry, but I can't."

"Faith, I—"

"I'll tell you this much—"

Then he interrupts my anger and says, "I love you. I hope to see you."

"Let me think about all this. If you pass through this way—"

"But you won't be home you said."

"Yes, I am going out of town. If you should call, it goes automatically to my cell phone. I will always get the call. That is all I can do for now. Goodbye." Then I slam the phone down onto my pain.

On autopilot, I walk into the kitchen, stoop down onto the linoleum floor, and reach far back into the corner of the bottom shelf. Hidden for years, its presence is never far away, even after twenty years of sobriety. It has sat there, daring me day after day to slip and open it up.

My hand embraces the bottle of Petite Syrah as I ignore the torrent of guilt tapping me on the shoulder. There is the anxious feeling while I dig in the kitchen drawer, searching for the unused corkscrew, then the aggression as I pierce the metal tip in the center of the cork and rotate down and downward until the familiar barrier is breached. I pull out the cork. Success! I pour the rich red fluid into a rose-colored iced tea tumbler. A sip, a swallow, and the warmth of the wine melts the tension in my shoulders and steadies my hand. The bottle has not been stored properly, and I detect a hint that it is turning. I'm just in time!

135

A smile of familiarity creeps onto my face as I hold the glass up to the sun coming in the window, watching the light change the wine into liquid pools of garnet gems. I contemplate pouring that second cup. After only one glass, I feel a welcome serenity. Nothing and no one exists but that beautiful red wine. *Hello, my old friend. How have you been all these years? I've missed you, too.*

Do I dare to pour another? I'm fine. What harm could it do?

Back in my drunken days, I would become so sick I had to live with mother. I hurt so bad at times I would vomit into a bucket. My mother would come and empty it.

Then one day, mother came into the house and said, "Faith, I have news."

"What?" I asked, barely listening. "I have a spot on my lung." From then on I watched my mother die in front of me. I could do nothing for her. So I kept drinking.

I drank so much back then that I couldn't even go to the hospital to visit. I was so ashamed. I doubted my worth and doubted that I could possibly be important enough to make any difference. In the end, she died while I was at the nearest bar.

When I finally staggered into the hospital after the bar closed, a nurse reported that she had died. I was so drunk I could barely stand. I went out to the car, reclined the seat, and passed out. I awoke when the sun shone in on my face, with a horrific hangover. It took a few minutes to realize where I was, then finally the vague memory that someone had told me that mother had died. Had I dreamt it? No. Her rings sat on the seat, the rings she never took off. Mother had died alone because I was busy getting drunk. She died worrying about me.

After mother's death, I entered my own personal recovery and fight every day to see the good I have inside. My illness wants to tell me otherwise. Looking back on that earlier time, I decided that a little more wine wouldn't do any harm. Just this once, to celebrate how far I have come.

"Let me take that. Please, Faith."

"Get away, Joseph. How the hell did you get in here anyway?" My head is pounding the drumbeat of my march to destruction.

Joseph waits silently by my side, as I fight my demons. I am furious that he intruded on this private scene that he has caught me.

And then in a powerful moment built on years of denial, I pull my head out of the sand.

"Damn it all!" I hurl the almost full wine bottle against the brick wall in the kitchen and watch it shatter, pieces of glass tinkling down onto the stone floor, flashing colors in the sunlight. The red wine has splashed into a wet star shape turning the brick to a burgundy color as it slowly dribbles along the lines of mortar.

"Devil, be gone!" Joseph shouts and pulls me into his arms, rocking me back and forth as I dissolve into a discordant melody of gasps, sobs, and screams.

There is a critical wink in our lives when we can make a terrible mistake if there is no one there who cares. In this, the worst juncture since I was fifteen, I almost lost myself again. If I've ever felt blessed, it was at that moment when Joseph walked in and became my guardian angel.

Chapter 23

The homeless on the streets, in shelters, and struggling in cheap motels with families, are our fellow human beings and could be any one of us.
—Debra Marie DeLash

Faith
Raleigh, North Carolina

The sun has risen over the city of Raleigh, and I'm feeling great anticipation for the people Joseph and I will meet at the homeless festival today. Disappointed after our board presentation last night, I question my ability to explain the shameless conditions and treatment of the mentally ill in jails. I so desperately want the decision-makers to understand.

Joseph says I doubt my own abilities and do not recognize my worth. Always quick to remind me, he often says, "Faith, you are strongest in your weakest spot. Believe in yourself as I do." That Joseph, he is a keeper.

The Homeless Kitchen sits on the corner of a run-down neighborhood in the older part of Raleigh. Decades ago, it was a hardware store in a thriving community of immigrants. The kitchen is partly funded by the nonprofit Loving1Home, donations from local churches, and this annual festival. Artists of all varieties are proudly displaying their paintings, cloth art, and calligraphy, hoping to sell their labors of love. Loving1Home shares the profit evenly with the artist. A community tradition for the past ten years, the festival shines a spotlight on the plight of the homeless and brings in much-needed money.

"Hey there, guys, back for another year?" Super Friend, as she is affectionately known in street circles, sports a hand forward. I feel warmth merely being in the same room with her.

Super Friend is a beautiful woman in her midfifties with black hair, which she wears tucked into a baseball cap. Homeless travelers nicknamed her Super Friend, as she is of a sensitive nature and able to quickly size up anyone in her path. This skill can be life-preserving when you live on the street. It is as important as air and water. To stay alive in this world, you must know who you can trust. Your survival depends on it. None of my friends know this about me, but I too lived on the streets while in my late twenties. I am one of the lucky ones who found a new life.

Days start early in the shelters. You must be up by 6:00 a.m., clean up, have your breakfast, and check out at 7:00 a.m. sharp. If you don't leave on time, you lose your place in line for a cot the next night. Before leaving the shelter each day, Super Friend must tuck her hair into this man's baseball cap. She says, "A girl must never look too much like a girl if you know what I mean." She grins, and the years lacking dental care stare back as wide, dark spaces where nature intended there to be teeth.

"I grew up with a parent who lived with mental illness," she explains to anyone interested. "My mother was diagnosed when I was little. She fought a relentless battle with long periods of depression and psychosis. Needless to say, I became the mother of my mother. Growing up, I was abused, neglected, and no one taught me how to care for my body, even basic health, and hygiene. Others take simple lessons such as this for granted."

But today, Super Friend is present and ready to help others. She once explained to me why she spends so much time with street people.

"I have lived with those who are damaged and troubled for so long. I don't really know how to relate to whatever normal is. It's where I'm supposed to be, I guess."

Ready to get the day going, I ask her, "Joseph and I will set up over here if that will work?"

"Sure, gal. Let me help you carry in the boxes."

Super Friend follows me out to the car. I lift out a box of pamphlets I intend to sell. These booklets are filled with literary contributions from many of the regulars who frequent the homeless kitchen. They write about where they came from mostly, in heartbreaking detail of lives most people will never understand. Sometimes, they are able to share their hopes and dreams for getting off the streets.

These are no ordinary stories.

Super Friend assembles their stories throughout the year and mails them to me. I print the pamphlets and add artwork from several of the Loving1Home artists. It is truly a smorgasbord of raw talent. One of the boxes appears to be missing from the car trunk, as well as the poster board I could have sworn I packed. I turn to Super Friend.

"Sorry, I am a bit distracted these days."

"I know, gal. Your usual spark, my friend, it seems to have taken a hike. Where did you lose it?"

I want to avoid talking about my father with anyone, even with Super Friend. I can barely acknowledge his existence myself.

"Let me grab this big box. There are enough booklets in there to set up." I lift the box and turn rather quickly, lost in growing anxiety. I forget to look where I am going and bump head-on into a man who looks as if he just stepped off the Brawny paper towel commercial. The booklets fall to the ground and scatter everywhere. As he helps pick up every last one, we strike up a conversation.

We begin by talking about what brought us here and turn to talk about our times of need. One of the many things I learn from people who find themselves homeless is their tendency to skip the small talk. He seems a bit defensive, does he think I see him as lazy? In a short time, my booth is set up thanks to this kind helper. Super Friend has taken off to check on the other booths.

The Brawny Man looks at me squarely in the eye and explains, "I am a hard worker, always have been. This is not the life I set out for. Was a mechanical engineer, registered even. Only a small percentage of engineers ever pass their licensing exams. But I did on the first try."

My eyes widen, and I begin to listen to what he has to say. I know I have fears about how others see me and understand his being defensive.

The room is now packed to the brim, mostly with people who are homeless mixed with a smaller group of community representatives, board members, and some curious onlookers. The latter try to fit in by dressing down, by not looking affluent. But the shoes always give them away. After all, hand-me-down shoelaces often don't match, and the homeless know well how to use duct tape to keep ill-fitting old shoes on their feet.

People at a gathering like this often approach me to ask how someone loses it all and ends up standing in the homeless line waiting for a meal. I must look more approachable than others. Giving an answer that will be understood by someone with good shoes is never easy. The Brawny Man continues his story as he fights back tears.

"I lost my whole family, first my wife, then my son. I had a big, beautiful home in a nice neighborhood and a wonderful life. In an instant, everything was gone.

"You see, it was hard to keep a job and spend weeks by my wife's side until she passed. Later, my son became sick, and I spent ten months at his bedside until he died. I lost my job because of time spent in the hospital. I had gone through vacation time, sick days, even compassionate leave without pay. How could I forsake them?"

Oh my god, what do I say to this? He looks at me, his eyes silently asking, "Please have some kind of answer."

All I could choke out of a tight throat was, "I'm sorry. I'm so very sorry."

The man is so deeply depressed, now sitting on a cardboard box with his head in his hands, motionless, his eyes glued to the floor. His silent cry goes unnoticed for the most part. The look of dejection is all too commonplace in this part of the city.

All that loss in a person's life, like childhood trauma, hell *any* trauma, it wreaks havoc with your brain chemistry. After the shock of the individual disaster passes, you think you are the same. But you cannot be. All you can do is fake it. Brawny Man continues to talk about his struggles and how much he wants to live again. He stands up to leave.

"You know, raising money to keep the kitchen open is righteous and all, but for me? The idea just doesn't work. Yeah, a meal is great; yet, I fight every day to find it within myself to just get up and keep going. I don't see the point of surviving when everything is lost. No one seems to care about that."

I reach out to embrace his hand, but he has disappeared into the crowd, no longer interested in sharing time with anyone, except his memories.

More people pour through the doors as the festival has risen to full swing in several hours. I always think it is a neat mixture of folks, some wearing clothes so old they are about to shred to pieces. Others shopping for bargain art are dressed in apparel straight from Macy's.

Joseph returns from his post at the sign-in desk and is about to collide with our dejected Brawny engineer. In typical Joseph style, he throws his arm around the fellow's shoulders. The man does not respond, neither moving closer nor jerking away. He just freezes, waiting for it to end. Such is the horror of depression. You become a nonentity, even to yourself.

From my own experience, one of the worst parts of living with a mental illness is the feeling that something is choking you around the neck. My cohorts and I would sit on the sidewalk, lie under the bridges, and wait in line for hours in hope of a bed and hot meal. As grim as that may sound, the worst part is watching people walk by ignoring your presence, a mere few feet from them. They have perfected the art of not seeing. You exist in a different dimension, forever invisible.

The gut-wrenching loneliness of knowing you do not have a home, a family, and anyone who gives a damn that you exist. If you don't show up somewhere, who would care? That old knowledge that someone is waiting for you is gone. Your existence, sitting on a curb, is completely insignificant. I shake off the creeping shadows and remind myself that I did escape alive. I now have a full life, and I have Joseph.

Our engineer, instead of leaving, returns to sit down on the floor next to our booth and watches the crowd. He has been there for hours now as people continue to tour the booths. Community members stop briefly at each table, some buying an art piece or a story. Most reach into their wallets to drop a few dollars into the donation jar set on each table.

I crouch down beside this man, careful not to let our bodies touch. People who live in fear do not like to be touched.

I whisper to him, "You know my body is like yours, always on high alert, fight or flight. It's the pits."

"Yeah," he quietly mumbles. That one word is the only thing he has said in hours, but it acknowledges a slight connection between two of the lost ones. Our day is coming to an end.

Super Friend returns to close out the booth. I have been so preoccupied, I hadn't noticed Joseph has sold out of pamphlets, and the festival is wrapping up. Normal people have done their duty and are heading home where someone is waiting for them. Most will forget the day before long. The guilt is depressing, and they will stuff the memory of homeless faces into a drawer.

Hearing the last of our conversation, his one word, Super Friend joins in.

"You know guys, I come here to help out, but I am always ready to run away. There is this inner space that feels I belong somewhere else. I call it a spiritual yearning in my soul."

Our engineer friend doesn't look up. Super Friend continues, "I took a bus trip years ago and passed through the Rocky Mountains. Looking at the majesty right in front of my eyes, how can I not believe in a creator. I just feel, if I am walking this earth thirsty, there must be something that will satisfy that thirst. Looking at all the people who have come across my path, their lives so hard, and full of sorrow, some have had grave injustices inflicted upon them. Well, if there is no justice for them in this life, there must be a better place. A spiritual kingdom of God, where justice will be done.

"I have lived a rough life and am old beyond my years and I can tell you, most of us? We are hungry for eternity. Deep down when we look through the clear lens I call spiritual eyes, one has to admit there is a god of the universe."

"I believe in God too. It is religion which chases folks away," I tell her.

"Oh Faith, that's only half of it. I have spent the past ten years going to different churches and talking to people who have had NDEs."

"Had what?"

"Near-death experiences. Do you know there are tens of thousands of documented cases just in the United States? This fascinates me. All these people experienced the spiritual realm. Comforting, isn't it?"

As she speaks, her eyes are twinkling, and I picture Dorothy setting out on the yellow brook road to find the heavenly kingdom. I decided to confide a deep secret of mine.

"You know, I have always been embarrassed to let people know I was once homeless. It happened during a rough patch, and my pride hasn't allowed me to tell anyone about those years. Not even Joseph knows the truth about my entire past."

"Hey, Faith. Don't beat yourself up. I see it in your eyes. Those times never really leave us. In my years, I have met hundreds of homeless people. And the majority? They live with either untreated mental illness, horrible life circumstance, or childhood abuse and abandonment."

I nod as I understand. It's almost a relief that she knows that I am no longer silently lying when I am with her.

"You know the worst?" I tell her. "It is the abandonment. There is this emptiness which you can never shake. As soon as I start to get close to someone, I begin doubting my feelings. Even with my special friend, Joseph, the ingrained distrust creeps out against my will. On some days, I worry how I will end up."

"Me too, Faith. This fear is why I travel from town to town. What am I driven by? The first thing I do when I reach a new place is to find directions to the local graveyard. If I walk by a field of flowers, I will pick as many bunches as I can carry. Then I spend time, walking up and down every aisle. I pause at every grave which is unmarked and count out a few flowers to place there. You see when homeless people die they are buried in unmarked graves."

"Yes, they would be, though I never thought about that aspect of their lives. There is no family to claim them or visit. They are faceless on the streets and eventually, even in death."

Super Friend pauses a moment and then in a hushed tone says, "When I die, I don't want my family nowhere. They have caused nothing but pain. I hate funerals when people cry and yet had nothing to do with the person while they were alive. Me? I'm donating my body to science. Super Friend will not be left in some unmarked grave. This past year, as I put flowers on the graves of the homeless, it was sadder than usual. Abandoned to death, as in life, unloved and unknown."

"But this isn't true." I add and am starting to tear up with the tragedy of it all, "Somewhere along the way, they had family and loved ones. Their lives must have meant something, even for a little while. After all, God wants us down here."

Super Friend continues, "Know what you mean about there being love and then the pain of abandonment. But I think when our time comes, we face our Maker on our own. We are born alone, and we die alone. I don't care what anyone thinks. It is not how we die or who is holding our hand when we die. It is how we loved that counts."

My cell phone interrupts our conversation. I look down at the number and then over at Joseph.

"It's him again, Joseph, my father. Why is he hounding me?"

"You know you don't have to answer it, dear. Tell me what you want to do."

"What do I want? I want him to stop. Isn't that what he did years ago? Stop loving me, that is?"

"Over there! Over there!" A woman's yell interrupts us, and I turn off the phone ringer, letting voice mail pick up his voice.

Out of nowhere appears a tall, lanky, and disheveled young man around mid-twenties. His eyes are frantic, and he is holding what appears to be a broken, metal leg off one of the cots at the shelter. All I see is a silver baton as it flies through the air.

"Snitches wear stitches! Snitches wear stitches!" He screams as he attacks our Brawny Man engineer still slouched on the floor.

Chaos ensues.

Super Friend yells at Joseph, "Call for Help! But come right back."

"Give me your phone, Faith," Joseph says, grabs it from my hand, and begins dialing 911.

The room fills with frantic ramblings; clearly, the stranger believes our engineer is the enemy. He is responding to commands from his auditory hallucinations. There will be no internal peace until he obeys.

"You told everyone my secrets. And now the army is coming to kill me!"

Our engineer tries to block the blows. He rolls into a ball and tries to squirm away. But the strength of the stranger's delusions is winning. There is a pool of blood forming beneath the engineer's arm where the aluminum leg made impact.

Historically, the police are slow to respond to disturbances at the shelter. They are far too common an occurrence. If there is an upstanding member of society in trouble, homeless calls take a back seat.

Super Friend cleverly sticks her leg out and catches the stranger's legs, and he pitches forward falling to the ground. The aluminum weapon which he had tightly gripped now slips from his fingers and skitters across the floor, where a woman plants her sneaker on top of it.

Joseph quickly drops the phone back into my bag and, with two other men, subdues the stranger. One of the men pulls duct tape out of his pocket and tapes the young man's hands behind him. Help in the form of a police car finally arrives two hours later. The other people in the hall that day either left the building when the fight started or stood on the sidelines to watch. For a long time, there was not much for spectators to see, as the young man had curled up on the floor and gone to sleep.

Because this episode is unusual in their lives, some can't resist watching the bizarre behavior. Watching, yes, but most in our society do not want to feel the pain. They live with the illusion that the homeless are "the others," not them. Or perhaps a person being homeless is somehow a result of bad luck, poor choices, or heavy drinking, something which is within their control if they would just try harder. Maybe it's better not to think about it at all.

Untreated mental illness is not a choice. Who would choose this life?

The police finally put the young man in the back seat of their car. Ironically, the Brawny engineer is put into another cop car; both are headed out to the nearest hospital with a psych ward. I turn to Joseph.

"Let's follow them. I want to make sure our engineer is treated properly. And the stranger? Maybe they will send him for treatment."

Joseph chuckles. "Sure thing, Faith. Miracles can happen, right? What the heck, let's go."

The Dorothea Dix Psychiatric Hospital is located on Dix Hill in Raleigh, North Carolina. It is named after mental health advocate of Victorian times, Dorothea Dix. I, too, have seen the inside of that same hospital when in my mid-forties and pray things have improved since then. Another story Joseph does not know.

Joseph and I quickly pack our boxes into the car and leave for the Dorothea Dix Hospital.

Chapter 24

In everyone's life, at some time, our inner fire goes out. It is then burst into flame by an encounter with another human being. We should all be thankful for those people who rekindle the inner spirit.

—Albert Schweitzer

Faith and Joseph
Dorothea Dix Hospital
Raleigh, North Carolina

The emergency department at Dorothea Dix hospital is overwhelmed. They take care of too many people with too little staff, which ends up herding those in trouble like cattle. Numerous, old uncomfortable metal chairs are filled with suffering souls, who are retching, coughing, holding a bloody appendage, or showing a host of other assorted maladies. One cannot walk among them without wondering what contagion is being passed around. Will some of us walk out sicker than when we came in? I won't give in to the impulse to run out the door.

Joseph and I thread our way through an assortment of those needing help toward the hopefully labeled "Help Desk." I am not feeling encouraged but ask the receptionist for information on the two men brought in from the shelter.

"Yes, ma'am. Your family was escorted in by police an hour ago. You folks can go back in the holding pen and wait with them if you really want to."

"In the what? Oh no, that is not necessary. I only want to check on their condition, that's all," Joseph pipes in quickly.

"Come on, Joseph. I know you want to do more than that," I tell him.

The receptionist pushes her glasses up her nose and looks at us both with undisguised fatigue. This query is taking more of her energy than she can afford to lose.

"As I said, psych patients are held over there for everyone's protection."

I look at where she is pointing, but all I see is dark shadows and bundles, people who have been waiting for God only knows how long.

Psychiatric patients are still kept in the back rooms, I see. Even the walls are a dingy aqua, a color popular in the fifties, left over from the days when patients were hidden away by embarrassed relatives. Apparently, lack of funds walked hand in hand with lack of caring. Just put the inconvenient out of sight and move on in one's now uncluttered life.

I could hear them before I saw them, the rows of the nameless and forgotten. Joseph and I reach the entrance to the holding pen. The hallway moans and complaints increase to deafening. Finally, on the third gurney from the left corner, I spot our delusional fighter from the shelter. He lies on his back, trapped in a drab, gray-restraint vest locked onto the gurney. Previous delusional rants have now been replaced with a smorgasbord of frustrated obscenities. Apparently, his neighbors are finding this distraction amusing and are competing with each other to unearth the most shocking words from their vocabularies.

"Where is our engineer?" Joseph yells out.

"Yeah, where is our engineer?" someone echoes helpfully.

"He's probably the only one who is not yelling. Let's follow the sound of silence, and I bet we find him."

A young man in handcuffs begins gently singing Simon & Garfunkel's, "Hello, darkness, my old friend."

And find him we did.

Brawny Man engineer sits hunched forward in a wheelchair, barely looking up as we call out his name. Someone has haphazardly wrapped a Kerlix bandage around his arm without securing it tightly.

Bloodstains soak through the gauze. I feel the word neglect hanging in the foul-smelling air.

"Where is the nurse, my friend?" I ask him.

Brawny Man's eyes suddenly pop wide open as double doors slam forward, with a male nurse and two huge male attendants exploding into the room. Stunned, we watch the nurse whisk out a large syringe and plunge the needle none too gently into our restrained young fighter's neck as he lies trapped on the gurney.

A small card drops from beneath his pillow as he rolls his head away to avert the attack. Curious, Joseph walks over to retrieve the card. The young fighter is already sliding into an artificial calm, his eyes closing.

"Look at this." Joseph shows us the card, which turns out to be a snapshot of two boys, one apparently the fighter in early teens wearing the same smile we saw earlier. Turns out our young fighter's name is Buzz. The other boy is slightly younger, maybe twelve. The photo identifies his name as Mark. Despite the worn and smudged photo, Mark has the brightest red hair I have ever seen. The two are obviously delighted as they both hang on to an adorable, wiggling new puppy. The edges of the picture are frayed and worn.

"I wonder who the younger boy is." Brawny man breaks his silence, reaching out for the picture.

I notice that blood continues to slowly seep out of the bandage and yell in exasperation at one of the attendants in the corner.

"Hey! This man needs some attention. His bandages are undone. Isn't there more help around here?"

One of the male attendants snaps back, "Ma'am, this is a triage situation. We have to attend to the most severe cases first. Your friend is medically stable. We know what we're doing."

I roll my eyes knowing nothing will make sense out of ridiculous and conflicting hospital rules. This frantic scene does not encourage independent thinking, only rushed, robotic reactions.

My phone's Beethoven's "Ode to Joy" ring interrupts, causing all those nearby to silence briefly the obscenity contest.

"Yes. Faith Goodwill here. Hello?"

"Hello, Miss Goodwill. My name is Frank."

"I'm in a noisy emergency room, sir. Can you call back later?"

"Well, you see, umm, it's just that. You know my grandfather, John Goodwill."

I stand there in silence, unable to believe that my father is involving his own grandson in this drama. I just can't deal with this. When will this nightmare go away?

"I can't do this now, Frank. Your grandfather called out of nowhere, and what does he expect, that the world will stop to accommodate his whim? I need time to deal with this, and right now is *not* the time."

Ready to exercise the wonderful power of pushing the OFF button to end this nonsense, I hear Frank snap, "Wait! He's running out of time."

"For God's sake, will you *please* get to the point?"

"Faith, this morning at 3:00 a.m., Grandpa was taken by MedFlight to the Boston Massachusetts General Hospital. They admitted him to the third floor, cardiac intensive care."

"Faith, quick! We need a doctor *now!*" Joseph catapults my thoughts away from the phone.

The Brawny Man is in the middle of a full-blown seizure. With a quick scan of the empty hallways, I know he is in trouble. There is not a professional in view. I let the cell phone and my connection with Frank drop to the ground. My sixty-year-old legs run into the emergency room, yelling for help at the top of my lungs.

I manage to gasp out, "Grand mal seizure, in there. Come!" A nurse and a young intern in blue scrubs follow my frantic trail back to our friend, now thrashing uncontrollably, his skin pale, wet, and clammy. The nurse pushes a roll of gauze from her pocket into his mouth and runs his wheelchair to a more secluded area, pulling shut the curtain.

Joseph and I stare at each other in astonishment.

"What happened?" Joseph looks confused as one moment Brawny Man was sitting peacefully looking at the photo, and the next he is in physical chaos.

We all know intellectually that life is fragile at its core. But even the most seasoned of us can be taken aback to see the reality of this truth played out. *How do nurses keep their sanity,* I wonder silently.

After an hour of pacing and checking on the young sleeping fighter, we finally see the nurse pulling back the curtain to leave Brawny Man's room. The nurse assumes Joseph and I are family as she breaks HIPAA privacy laws, pausing to explain his condition. The situation appears under control, and our friend is now resting comfortably with an IV in place and an oxygen mask over his mouth. His arm is properly bandaged. He finally looks comfortable.

One of the patients from the hallway enters carrying a thin blue hospital blanket for Brawny Man. He gently covers this stranger, whom apparently he cares about. Brawny Man looks up at him and speaks.

"Thanks, man. I am a bit cold, the blanket sure feels good."

The nurse turns to us. "He will be fine. A seizure, possibly brought on by dehydration and lack of nutrients. No food, no good. The stress of the fight also may have triggered this. I gave him a dose of ketamine, and he is already responding well."

"Ketamine?" Joseph asks.

"It's generally for acute depression, but it has other uses. He really needs to eat more often. Basically, this whole episode is about severe low blood sugar," she explains and turns promptly to respond to a patient screaming, "Damn it, Mother!" over and over from the hallway.

I turn to Joseph, "Eat more often? Doesn't anyone get it? One cannot eat food that isn't there."

Chapter 25

It's a journey unfinished, Faith. Don't look too hard
for answers right now. It will become clear to you
in God's time, not necessarily when you want it to.
                                    —Debra Marie DeLash

Faith and Joseph
Dead Broke Farm
Raleigh, North Carolina

"Joseph, this is such a great escape from the stress. I have always wanted to try my hand at horseback riding." There is a bus ahead of us carrying a group of thirty-or-so-fifth-grade students. I maneuver our rental car into the tight vacant spot between the bus and a brand-new BMW.

"Careful, dear," Joseph warns, "you are awfully close to that Beemer."

"Trust in my abilities, won't you?" I chuckle and realize Joseph knows so little about my abilities and past inabilities. It is time to take a step forward in recovery and trust my friend. I need to open up that secret part I have carried for so many years in shame and expose my own failings to the light.

Located in Raleigh, Dead Broke Farm offers a hundred and ten acres of wooded riding trails, where sixty-five horses of varying experience levels wait to take people out into nature. I decide on a calm, older horse named Pablo, distinct with his creamy beige coat and beautiful sienna brown dots from head to tail. I walk up and pet Pablo's cheek while blowing gently into his nostrils so he could understand who I am. I would never have known this "secret handshake" if Joseph had not shown me. Pablo seemed to appreciate good manners and was patient as one of the grooms helped me up into the saddle. Joseph, the risk taker, had chosen Trigger, a lively young colt. The horses are obviously happy they have been chosen to leave the corral.

Around the main part of the farm, wandered contented ducks, turkeys, roosters, and a black standard poodle named Honey. They all seem quite used to each other, and Honey has obviously never learned to chase the chickens, which adds to the peaceful atmosphere.

Majestic, ancient oak trees line the road as we ride out the path away from the school kids and visitor's barn. Joseph convinced those in charge that we do not need a guide, so we are soon alone under the trees shading the path from both sides, meeting over the center of the trail, like a gothic cathedral arch. The sun filters down, through the leaves as we grow quiet, listening to the birds and skittering of occasional squirrels. Joseph finally interrupts my silence.

"Faith, you are going to explode if you don't talk."

"What if I wake up to discover I am my father. I mean we share the same genes. His blood is my blood, right?"

We ride quietly as the words search for a place to rest. The horses seem to sense my anxiety, occasionally unsettled in their stride, finally wandering off the path to nibble grass. Joseph guides Trigger to nudge Pablo back onto the trail.

"Dear, you are nothing like your father. I can't imagine you being capable of abandoning anyone who needed you. You are kind. You are trusting. You are Faith."

"No Joseph, no, no. As it turns out, I probably am my father's daughter. I need to share some things that just have not come up. Been too private, too scared to let anyone see all of me."

"Oh boy, that sounds mysterious."

"No, it isn't anything ominous, just things I have not been proud of and hid from. There's a saying, 'Fake it 'til you make it.' I've been guilty of pretending to be normal until I could finally feel comfortable in the role, and it became part of me. It was actually advice one of the psychiatrists gave me a long time ago, one of the rare bits that stuck in my brain.

"I was twenty-three and had just relapsed from heroin. Mom had me admitted to the hospital. Well back then, I detoxed and completed their thirty-day program. I even received a new diagnosis, Manic–depressive illness. I had been labeled schizophrenic and lived with that stigma for many years. Suddenly, I had a new diagnosis, one that seemed less scary."

"I understand how freeing that must have been. Go on, Faith."

Joseph grabbed Pablo's reins and simultaneously guided him and Trigger under a large oak tree to rest and get some water. I sat down in the shade next to Joseph.

"Mom paid for my hospital stay with bank savings accumulated from her cafeteria job at the local nursing home. She worked the terrible night shift, in a cheap, smelly facility where the moans of residents echoed the hallways. She said those were the darkest hours for mostly lonely people, who felt no one cared about them. Somehow she understood how unfair it was that they had just been left there alone. No one came to visit. She called it, 'A warehouse for the dying.'

"Well, it was the day of my discharge, and the social worker had set up a ninety-day residence in a transitional house.

"Mom was excited. After all, it was supervised housing and mental health counseling. I think she believed that magic would happen, and I would be cured. That morning, mom had stopped by the bank and pulled out the last of her money."

"Your mom sounds like an amazing woman."

"Yes, but let me finish before the words stick in my throat. An hour before mom was to arrive, I took the $100.00 I had hoarded in my bottom dresser drawer in a pair of socks, put all my belongings in a red-checkered backpack, and I ran! Down the ramp of the hospital, onto the main road. I stuck out my thumb to hitch a ride, praying I could make a getaway before someone caught me.

"An old, blue Beetle Bug with painted amateurish daisies pulled up, full of hippie-types. A guy in the front passenger seat rolled down his window. He had curly blonde shoulder-length hair needing a shampoo, over a black Grateful Dead T-shirt. He asked with an amazingly deep voice, 'Where are you headed?'

"'Anywhere away from here,' I answered. 'Can you help with gas money?' 'I have a little, not much,' I told him, waiting for him to make up his mind. 'Okay, hop in.' He turned around and told a girl with an almost shaved head, 'Angie, can you make room back there for—what's your name, kid?'

"Angie opened the back door, scooted over silently, as I answered, 'Faith.' I shoved my backpack under the seat where there were other backpacks, empty fast food containers, and a few magazines. He said they were headed toward California to a place called Big Sur. They were eager to get to a famous ocean view hang out called Nepenthe.

"It only took a few minutes in the VW bug to forget about mom waiting with only the receipt from the savings she had withdrawn. What kind of person does that to her own mother?"

"You were not the same person you are now. Give yourself a break, Faith. Go on."

"So, I rode with my new amigos, three older boys and a girl my age. Three people in the backseat of a VW bug is a tight squeeze. We had to get friendly, like it or not. They were passing around a quart of Cuervo tequila with salted lime halves, smoking joints, and taking turns driving. It was a miracle we didn't get busted. We would have done serious jail time.

"They had a little heroin, mostly grass. It was bliss. Josh, the guy with blonde hair, had big green eyes. You know what a sucker I am for green eyes. Well, once we got out to the California coast, we headed south to the Monterey Peninsula and Big Sur. Josh pitched a tent for just the two of us. The others disappeared to another place in the campground. I think the other girl might have been interested in Josh before I came along but seemed to give him up without blinking, so I didn't worry about it. We were all too stoned to care about rules and territory, even quit caring that his hair needed washing.

"The next night, the main driver, Bill, came to our tent with some heroin he had scored at Nepenthe, and it was party time. I don't think I ever got to the famous landmark.

"Every day Josh would inject me with heroin, and I would just lie there and float. Before long, I didn't care what he did, the feeling of giving over complete control. Oh my god, I was in ecstasy.

SEEKING MY DAUGHTER FAITH

"What happened to mom? I called her once from the road. I don't remember a word of the conversation, except she was crying, and that was a bummer I didn't want to hear, so I hung up.

"As I became enmeshed with Josh and the drugs, my reality faded into sweet oblivion. I can imagine the living hell mom was enduring. She lost her daughter and her life savings in one day."

I became quiet, with the only sounds heard from Trigger and Pablo slurping water from a recent rain puddle. Joseph reached out to hold my hand in silence, waiting for the story to continue.

"Joseph, you know what was the most addicting? I had found a group of people who accepted me for all my flaws, and we stuck up for each other. There was a misguided loyalty among us, glued together by drugs. I craved the support and unconditional love I had not felt since I became sick, and the perpetual haze convinced me that I finally found what was missing."

I wipe my nose on my sleeve and look off to the horizon as if to escape the awful place my story revisited.

"Mom somehow tracked me down where I was living and one day to my shock showed up at the door. I learned the power of genuine, inexplicable forgiveness, and I finally entered a transitional housing program.

"Mom taught me that storms in life will continue to come, but I was growing a strength day by day that would see me through. It was not magic, like a bright light illuminating the dark; it was more like a slow sunrise, barely noticeable from moment to moment.

"Well, I found that strength, Joseph, but it has been a slow climb. I had to learn about making good decisions and about not running away when things got sticky. I have always wondered about my father if he struggled as I have. Are we more alike than I ever wanted to admit? It's confusing, and I don't know how I feel at this point."

Fighting tears, I stand up and walk over to remount my patient Pablo. Before Joseph led us back out onto the trail, he turns to me and finally comments on my sad history.

"It's a journey unfinished, Faith. Don't look too hard for answers right now. It will become clear to you in God's time, not necessarily when you want it to. I know that's a cliché, but clichés come into being because they are true. I think something positive is going to come out of this, despite how insurmountable the problem seems now. Follow the name your father gave you, Faith, and have faith."

Chapter 26

When I finally accepted that he was really gone, I had a choice. I could either die or find my own path and to hell with him.

—Debra Marie DeLash

Faith and Joseph
Dorothea Dix Hospital
Raleigh, North Carolina

After a couple day's rest, Joseph and I stop by the hospital to say goodbye to our new friends. I am impressed by their renewed appearance.

"Hey, thought we would swing by on our way back to Maine. It's amazing what seventy-two hours of good food, a hot shower, and medical attention will do. Looking good, my friend."

Though Brawny Man has perked up, I dread his return to the street life. His release is imminent as he is not a danger to himself or others and thus, will not meet criteria for continued care. Unfortunately, he will fall through the cracks. Brawny Man looks my way, "I feel more human. That's for sure. And the man who attacked me in the shelter? Seems his name is Buzz. Turns out now that he is on meds, is quite the good guy. He came in last night with a Monopoly game he lifted from the recreational therapy room."

Joseph pulls up a stool and sits down.

"Remember the picture Buzz dropped onto the floor the other day? Well, there was a phone number scratched on the back."

"And if you know my Joseph, there is no way he is going to leave that one alone."

Brawny Man nods.

Joseph proud of his detective skills continues to explain.

"Turns out the younger boy in the picture is Buzz's brother, Mark. In his late thirties, Mark is a businessman right here in the suburbs, does mostly contracts to build vessels of some sort. Buzz's family has been frantically looking for him ever since last Christmas when he took off following dinner. According to Mark, Buzz doesn't grasp the reality that he needs medicine. So he doesn't take it, and the family wrings their hands and watches helplessly as Buzz gets sicker and sicker. Then they find him only when he ends up in an emergency room."

"Yeah," Joseph continues, "the brother sounds like a decent guy. Buzz's seventy-two-hour hold is up today, just like yours. Mark is coming to pick him up."

"Wow, guys, you have been busy," Brawny man chuckles.

Joseph explains, "Connecting with people keeps one in recovery, my man."

"Did I hear someone mention my name?" Buzz's brother, Mark, enters wearing Docker khakis and an Izod polo shirt. Buzz is by his side, dressed in clean scrubs from the hospital. Brawny Man greets the two men.

"You look like your picture, a bit older perhaps, but still, have the red hair. Met your brother at the shelter." Brawny Man extends his hand to Mark in friendship, who shakes it firmly, and says, "What is your name sir?"

Brawny Man looks embarrassed. "I can't remember the last time someone asked my name. My name is Stephen, Stephen Banks."

"Nice to meet you, Stephen. Are you from these parts?"

"No, just passing through. Been passing through for the past couple years. Before that lived in New York. I worked as an engineer." Brawny Man, now Stephen, states.

"Engineer?" Mark asks.

"Yep, that's right. Twenty years, mostly vessel work. Not lately though."

He glances over at Buzz.

"Life can really get in the way," Buzz replies.

"Yup," Stephen answers.

"Ready, bro? I am ready to spring this joint." Buzz moves in toward Mark, clearly building up a bit of anxiety. As Buzz begins to reach to open the curtain, his brother hesitates a moment, then turns toward Stephen.

"Stephen? I have a question. My company recently got a new contract. We have orders to build several large vessels over the next few years and are looking for qualified engineers. If you're interested in a job, I can get you an application."

Brawny Man's face brightens, suddenly looking ten years younger as he hops off the table.

"I have to be honest. My last job? I was so stressed that one day I just walked out, haven't worked since. Better know this up front."

Buzz walks up beside his brother. He stops his pacing.

"Hey, Stephen, Mark here gave me a second chance. Look at all the trouble I've caused him. He continues to forgive my escapades. Maybe, my comrade, you deserve another chance too."

Mark leans in and puts his arm around his brother. Stephen hesitates and then takes a leap of faith.

"I accept the kindness. Thank you, sir."

Mark places his business card in Stephen's hand and explains, "After a good night's rest, show up at the address listed here. The office is right on the bus line. Ask for me at the front desk, and together, we'll go get you an application."

"Come on, brother, we need to get you some clothes that fit. I think you've lost a bit of weight."

The two brothers now pull back the curtain and arm in arm head for the door under the EXIT sign.

Brawny Man, or Stephen from this day forward, packs up the few toiletries given by the hospital, shakes our hands, and heads for the same exit door. I could swear I saw tears in his eyes as he turns away. He plans to get a cot in the shelter tonight before the beds fill up. The dreadful aqua doors have now closed behind them as we stand there catching our breaths.

Joseph grabs my hand and gives it a squeeze.

"Life is short but fascinating, isn't it, my dear?"

"I know, Joseph. But remember that call the other morning, when I dropped the phone on the floor? Well, it was my father's grandson of all people. Father has taken quite ill and is in intensive care. He thought I would want to know."

"Faith, my love, you doubt yourself far too often. I have seen this in you, yet you are strong and brave despite the fear."

"Oh, Joseph, you silly old fool."

"Dear, if you don't go to see your father, I believe you will always regret it. Giving someone a second chance? Maybe it is not so much about them as about us. You deserve to go, Faith. You deserve the freedom that forgiving your father will bring to your life."

"Maybe you are right, but it may be too late. The hospital is over a thousand miles away. That is two straight days of driving. Arriving too late might be even worse."

"You could fly, dear."

"And pay with what, my good looks? You know money is tight. A last-minute flight will be several hundred dollars that I don't have."

Joseph reaches into his back pocket and retrieves his wallet.

"Remember in all the commotion the other day? I was the one who picked up the phone off the floor. I talked to Frank. In all the chaos, you didn't know I listened to the message he left afterward. Here take this and split! You have to try, dear. Get a taxi to the airport and hop on a plane."

Joseph counts out four one-hundred-dollar bills. I notice his left wrist is striped where the tan ends, and something is missing.

"Joseph, where is your gold bracelet, the one your uncle gave to you? You never go anywhere without it." Joseph smiles and his eyes sparkle.

"Oh, go on now, dear. You have bigger fish to fry than worrying about where my bracelet is. Have a safe trip, and remember, my heart goes with you."

I am overwhelmed with love for this blessed companion, as I dart for the infamous aqua exit. For an instant, I think the sign should really say, ENTRANCE, to announce the portal into changed lives for those who walk through it.

My fear of flying will have to take a hike. The adrenaline is pumping, my heart still pounding, as I hail a taxi to the airport. I am mere hours away from seeing my father after forty-five years. I don't know if I'm more scared to see him or terrified I will be too late. *God, help me. Am I doing the right thing?*

The airport waiting room expands in the silence as I recall my father taking me at seven years old to watch the horse shows at the circus. I would sit mesmerized as the ringleader led the horses around the ring in their slow, measured gait. Father would place his arm on my shoulder, and I felt protected, safe from any evils that might come. Yet, in a short few years, I could no longer hear my Father or anyone else for that matter. I walked into my teenage years, and suddenly, I was lost, alone.

My father used to say that if in your lifetime you have one or two friends who stick through thick and thin, you are indeed fortunate. When he left me at fifteen, he demonstrated clearly he was not one of those people who would stay. When I finally accepted that he was really gone, I had a choice. I could either die or find my own path and to hell with him.

Well, that was then. My flight has been called, and there is no turning back. Can I let go of the past and give him a second chance? It won't be easy, but a life lived with regrets is far worse.

Chapter 27

We are not human beings having a spiritual expe-
rience; we are spiritual beings having a human
experience.

—Pierre Teilhard de Chardin

Faith
Boston Massachusetts General Hospital

Flying is not part of my script. It costs money, you get jammed
in with people you don't like, there are delays and incon-
veniences, and the bathrooms smell funny. But here I am,
finally letting go of the armrest, working circulation back into my
white-knuckled fingers. Actually taking off was kind of fun, my version of a roller coaster. It's probably safer, but I won't spend a lot of
time thinking about that, will I?

Nervous about this wild goose chase, I ask the flight attendant
for some hot tea, which usually is relaxing to my spirit. Bored with
the puffy cotton cloud cover under the plane, I try to sleep.

"Here's your tea, madam. Would you lower your tray, please?"

I was already dozing and quickly drop the tray. The man in the
next seat is working on his laptop and obviously finds the attendant's
interruption annoying. He has already glanced toward my hippy
attire and finds me beneath his further notice. Get over yourself. I
am in no mood for big business ego.

I can feel myself slipping into much-needed sleep before the
tea cools. The engine sound of the plane reminds me of riding in the
back seat of father's car on the way to kindergarten.

I had only been to the school a month, but it seemed like my whole life, and I knew I didn't like it. There were mean kids who pulled my pigtails, untied the bow in the back of my dress, or hid my coat in the cloakroom. They lived to pick on me. I cried and cried every morning, begging not to go to school. But mother and father said things like, "You have to. It's the law." What law? What difference does it make if I go or stay home? I can read already, so why do I have to go somewhere else?

My father would pull up his car in front of the school entrance. It was an old building, made of red brick, with lawn and old trees all around. Lots of small-paned windows held different artwork by the kids. I might have liked the place if it were not for the bratty boys, who would wait for me on the steps with mean smiles. My father's arm reached over the front seat to hand over my Snoopy lunch box. Father was wearing his suit for going to work. He asked if I had the usual: sweater, pencil box, etc. It was the same list every day. Don't ask me why he kept doing it, but I answered politely because it made him happy. I shook the lunch box, trying to tell what's inside, and because it always annoyed him, making him say, "Don't do that. All the food will get mixed up, and you will have an apple sandwich and peanut butter to drink!" He loved that joke, so I laughed at it, every day.

"Did you write me a secret coded message?"

"Of course, Faith, don't I always?"

"Yes, Daddy. What does it say today?"

"You will need your decoder to find out. Do you have it in your shoe, as usual?"

"Yes, Daddy. If I'm not careful, one of those boys will get it."

"Don't worry, Faith. They will get bored and pick on someone else before long. Just ignore them."

The dream fades as the sound of the descending engines penetrates my sleep. I look out just in time to see the plane dropping down toward the end of the runway. I don't want the plane to land any more than I wanted to go to kindergarten. I'm a grown-up now. How come I still have to do stuff I don't want to?

I only have one carry on, fortunately. I scoot right by the tired, the poor, and other huddled masses through the endless corridors of the airport, following the sign to baggage, then out to grab a taxi. The driver stands politely to hold open the rear door of his lime green cab, sweeping me in with his right arm. Manners! What could go wrong with a driver with manners? Besides, he wears a beautifully wrapped turban.

I have read that the Sikhs are both a warrior tribe and the gentlest men on earth. It gives one a warm fuzzy feeling to ride behind one of them. The dashboard holds photos of two beautiful boys. He places my carry-on inside and gets into his seat in front. I am escorted into the back seat but behind the passenger seat so he can turn and talk. How thoughtful.

"Where may I take you, dear madam?"

"Massachusetts General Hospital, please."

"Ah, yes indeed, I know it very well, madam. My eldest son was born there." Manners and charm. I might be in love.

He pulls out from the airport curb and immediately passes two other taxis accelerating as if in Nascar. I assume this is the driving style in this city and try to unclench my hands. He has launched a description of his "beautiful and saintly wife's" labor pains in giving birth to his son. He frequently turns his head to see if I am listening with appropriate fascination. Apparently, he can see traffic out the back of his head. He comes too close, and other taxi horns honk; a few drivers shake their fists, but he is oblivious as he plunges ahead.

We are leaving the light industry and airport area and entering a maze of city streets with many high rises. Though a Sunday, traffic is ramping up into morning rush hour. Are all these folks going to church?

My driver occasionally curses in whatever Indian dialect he speaks, swerving around other vehicles and pedestrians. At one point I had to put my hands over my face and not look, as he flew down a one-way street, the wrong way. He turns, while still going the wrong way, and explains, "This is one of my most favorite shortcuts. It takes off at least ten minutes, you know." He waits until I remove my hands from my face and nod, accompanied by a sick smile, before he turns back to the road in time to pull up in front of the hospital! Miracle of miracles we are there.

He gets out, opens my door, hands over my carry-on, and actually does a perfect military salute. All this after I pay what's on the meter, plus a generous tip for getting me there alive. I say thank you, as I run in the door of the hospital.

Chapter 28

Your most profound and intimate experiences of worship will likely be in your darkest days—when your heart is broken, when you feel abandoned, when you're out of options, when the pain is great and you turn to God alone.

—Rick Warren

Grandfather
RV on the Road

I woke up on this ordinary Wednesday morning with absolute certainty that my life has changed permanently, from now to my death. Those self-revelations come rarely, and how we face them says a great deal about our character. We can deny, rage, cry, sink into depression, or accept with resignation. A rare few can accept with joy.

Before I open my eyes, I say the Serenity Prayer, knowing I could *accept the things I cannot change* that had been in process for the duration of my quest. I could even find *the wisdom to know what my stuff is* and what belonged to someone else. The hard one is the middle line: *Courage to change the things I can*. I had defined the quest and sought the journey; now, could I find the courage to carry it all out?

Frank has finished putting away the breakfast dishes in the RV kitchen, and I could hear him talking on the phone. He sounds a bit melancholy. I no longer feel concern about who is on the other side of the line, as I did only a few days prior. I haven't the strength to fight his battles, and it wouldn't help him if I did. A weird detachment, moving away from things I cannot explain nor control. I am connected to life only through that room in my heart which belongs to my Faith.

Not feeling well, I hid in bed all day yesterday and told Frank I needed to finish Faith's letter. But that is only a portion of the truth. I didn't want my grandson to discover I am lightheaded, breathing quite heavily, with a growing tension in my chest. Frank and I are so close these days that he would spot trouble in an instant. Traveling the country in a small RV will do that to a relationship. I have always loved Frank, but our lives were not shared authentically until we each confessed our secrets. Today, my grandson looks at me with love. But intimate exposure gives an insight into my health no one else has. This is a mixed blessing for an old man.

Drat! Who would have thought the pain of seeing my grandson's face when I tell him I am sick would be worse than the mounting pain which now radiates down my arm?

"Grandpa! Grandpa! Wake up, please, open your eyes!" This is one of the last things I remember. The other is the taste of salt as perspiration flowed into my mouth.

*****

Grandfather
Boston Massachusetts General Hospital

"What the hell? Where am I?"

"No worries, mate. You're nowhere near hell, or heaven for that matter. For now, you have landed in the hospital, third floor intensive care, the serious floor, which means we will tolerate no jokes out of you, my friend."

I hear an absurd sound which jolts me back to reality. It appears this man standing in front of me is singing, though the sound is unlike anything I'm in the mood to hear. He's doing a very bad impression of Nat King Cole, "Mona Lisa, Mona Lisa, they have named *youuuu*."

"Could you please shut up? I am sporting quite the headache. Who are you anyway?"

"Chaplain Charlie at your service."

Chaplain Charlie stands five feet ten inches I'd estimate, with wavy gray hair and a matching mustache which could use a major trim. He wears black scrubs and E width red tennis shoes. Draped around his neck is a handwoven Guatemalan stole, blinding with its bright blues, reds, oranges, and chartreuse. Where are the sunglasses in this place? Why do they let people in to torment those who are already hanging by our last thread?

"Chaplain? I am a lost cause, sir. I've never had much time for God."

"Nonsense. We all believe in something. We each just have a different name for things."

The more he talks, the more I realize his philosophy did not come out of a standard seminary textbook. He clearly walks a fine line between God and his personal view of the universe, which includes a skepticism of psychology and questionable reliance on theological approaches. There is something about him. He is both unique and unexpected.

Chapter 29

Old truths are always new to us if they come with the smell of heaven upon them.

—John Bunyan

Chaplain Charlie

My father was a physicist, one of the early ones who played with atomic energy. He was always flying to mysterious places and doing secret things. He sported the unique middle name of Justice, a silent hero figure.

Mother says he named me the day I was born. She wanted Oliver, but the great physicist came up with the unlikely name of Charlie. Mother said, "You mean Charles, of course."

"No, I mean *Charlie*," he said with assurance. They rarely argued, and she let him have his way, this time.

Not that my mother was lily-livered, she had been a high school math teacher until I was born, then stayed home. I'm not at all sure that is what she should have done, but apparently, she thought it was the right thing. With my father being gone so much, she ran the household with an iron hand, in a velvet glove. I knew she loved me, and I also knew who the boss was.

We lived in a little town in Kansas, and when I saw *Wizard of Oz*, I was so impressed that I determined to be the wizard when I grew up. Only I wasn't going to be the jerk that he was. I was going to take care of the Munchkins and tame the flying monkeys, and a lot of do-gooder things.

My parents went away for weekends occasionally, and I got to stay overnight with my best friend, Rich. Rich's parents would go to church camp meetings that were boisterous with loud preaching. I was expected to tag along. In the car, Rich would whisper, "Don't take anything too seriously. We just have to listen a while, and then we get to go out and play baseball." I would have put up with anything to play baseball. I figured that these Sunday meetings were on a par with washing your hands before dinner.

In school, I was better at what was called liberal arts than the sciences, barely getting through arithmetic. As for algebra, when I hit high school, forget it. The algebra teacher went home with a headache after having me in class every day. I wanted to know how Pythagoras arrived at those theorems, but the teacher would just say, "Never mind, just memorize and use it." This made no sense, and I dug my heels in. After taking the class twice, the teacher bribed me with a C- if I would never take the class again. After all those years, it occurred to me that maybe he didn't *know* the answer himself.

By the time I reached thirteen years of age, my reading had increasingly wandered into theology and the Bible. I would tell my parents, "I just love the history," and read the Old Testament with a flashlight under the covers at night. I often had several church history books open on my desk, along with a couple translations of the Bible.

My mother knew about this uncommon behavior but kept quiet. She had the attitude that my life had its own path and assignments, and I should not be interfered with. My father also understood without saying a word, being strong in his own beliefs. He would say, "Charlie, we are spiritual beings on a human journey." People often did not accept father's message, with mother explaining he was destined to be born in a different time.

Fortunately, my grades, other than algebra, were decent, and I went right to the local college after high school. I chose an early class in theology and, from that point, devoured the Bible and accepted I admittedly was considered unique. Father had been assigned to some mysterious government place of high secrecy in the desert, and we were not allowed to ask questions. He briefly raised the subject of our moving nearer to his new laboratory, but mother calmly told him that was not going to happen.

"We must put Charlie's education first. We just can't pull up stakes and move to the desert, abandoning all the work he has put in."

Father gave in, naturally. He was all left brain and, when confronted with mother's right-brained logic, would smile. Whatever he was working on, it must have been earth-shaking, because when I later announced I was going to seminary, he said very little.

Having done enough studying to determine with my usual arrogance that the church wasn't doing it right, I was going to fix their problem. I had been to enough churches to realize how far they had evolved from their roots which were to open a door in anyone's heart to the heavenly Father. Precious worship time was devoured with fundraising and social and financial reports. They claimed that one must enter "this" door on Sunday to find God, but it was not true. I believed in razor-sharp focus on the teachings of Christ, his Sermon on the Mount, and how he reacted to injustice and hypocrisy. He loved the forgotten among us and took the wiles of the enemy very seriously. I thought Christ was radical, a rebel, which shocked the seminary professors. I was threatened with expulsion more than once, and I had to pretend to go along with their approach.

Somehow they let me graduate, and I was ordained. Assigned to a small-town Anglican church in the northwest, I bid farewell to my blessed mother and drove off to Idaho in an old Studebaker. I had a letter approving my hiring and directions to the rectory. The house was old stonework, and exceedingly drafty in the snowy winters, but I adjusted. After all, Kansas was hardly the tropics either.

I soon found out that the home office in jolly old England had very definite traditions on what would be taught and when, sermon subjects, rituals, and more rituals. It isn't that I did not respect old rituals, but it seemed that an overly sacred aura was laid upon these things, even more than the study of Christ. Rituals first, Jesus later. When I would try to expand a bit and teach Jesus as I saw him, one of the old timers would rat me out to the bishops, and I would receive letters, then phone calls, then a personal visit from not one but two bishops. I was warned to toe the line, or else. The threat hung in the air, undefined.

I had a friend who was going to Guatemala for three days, and I was invited to go along. I took a weekend off and went. A few days turned into a month. I saw pure and beautiful faith living in the hearts of those in a tiny village, one that had no church. Yet they believed and followed Christ's example to love one another. I couldn't help confronting my crisis of church, though not a crisis of faith. My faith was unshakable, but I felt the church was governed by fear, man-made rules, and above all occupied with protecting itself. Somehow Christ's teachings and philosophy on how to treat our fellow human beings were stuffed into a dark file somewhere, rarely to see the light of day. I longed to stay with these people of less complicated faith, but I knew this would be running away. I eventually went back home and to my job.

I was later transferred elsewhere in the country, more than once, as I was unable to find the humility to color between the lines. One would think that loving the Father, the Son, and the Holy Spirit would suffice.

Scanning through a church periodical one day, something unusual caught my eye. A hospital in the northeast was looking for a chaplain. It was the last thing I would ever have thought of. But the ad jumped out at me as if God, Himself, had lit it up with red neon. I made a phone call, mailed off a questionable resume, and was invited for an interview. I had to borrow the plane fare from my mother, but I made the flight. There I found a surprising meeting of minds with the hospital administrator, who shared my belief that a chaplain's duty was to love and care for anyone who needed it.

I think people overuse the expression "sent by God," but this time, I really believed it. My work at the hospital is the most rewarding thing I have ever done. At a time when people are in extreme psychic and physical pain, I know I can help them in this part of their journey. Sometimes they come to me without faith, but they rarely leave without it. Isn't that what I was called to do? I should say so.

Chapter 30

Deep wounds penetrate into the core of being. There comes a moment where we can choose to turn it all around: no more hiding, secrets, or guilt. We can confess.

—Debra Marie DeLash

Grandfather
Massachusetts General Hospital

The one redeeming quality about landing in Massachusetts General Hospital intensive care is that I am thoroughly enjoying Chaplain Charlie's company. In fact, he is pulling me out of my personal doldrums with a totally different view than I have ever encountered. The walls I put up against God's salesmen are crumbling down.

We had several visits over the last couple days. He would show up at all hours, without warning or invitation. But when summoned by his enforcer, as he calls the hospital beeper, he would cuss in a decidedly un-chaplain-like manner yet run to answer the call with great purpose. Like the legendary postman, nothing stays this chaplain from his appointed rounds.

I am scared, resigned, yet focused, all at the same time. Is that even possible? All the MDs, residents, and interns enter and quickly exit my room after each has noted on my chart clipped to the foot of the bed. Sometimes they would take a moment to explain something. Mostly I would be ignored, as an inconsequential blob in the bed that holds the chart. I don't think anyone warns them in medical school that treating patients means they are treating human beings.

If I could get just one message out to all the MDs on the planet, it would be that folks, *kindness matters*!

Poor Frank, being the only relative present and my medical spokesman, is forced to endure this torture. As the hours tick on, I know my grandson needs to escape this mess. He's been babysitting since I was admitted here and is looking like he was just dumped out by a tornado. I suggest he escape to the cafeteria, but he doesn't move out the door.

This afternoon, the pulmonary specialist enters just as Chaplain Charlie arrives with his chessboard. My lungs are a disaster, and I am not prepared for what happens next. The pulmonologist barely greets Frank, Chaplain Charlie, or me. He scrolls hastily through his laptop to find the report on my lung capacity test.

"I see here you have had several small strokes, sir. And your lungs are in terrible condition. The pneumonia is worsening. Clearly, all the antibiotic trials have not cleared the infection."

"Uh-huh." Frank looks like he is about to pass out. Poor kid.

"You are getting weaker. Not sitting up to try and clear out your lungs? They're sounding bubbly, with fluid. We will need to start mechanically clearing this out."

"What does this mean? Why?" Frank asks.

I already know the answer. The pulmonologist continues, addressing Frank as a lecturing professor.

"We can clear this fluid out, but I believe it will continue forming. Unfortunately, this provides a haven for bacteria and germs. He will die drowning in fluids."

This cold fish says all that with total detachment, ignoring me as if I were an insensate mouse in the corner.

"Isn't there a better way to go than this?" I ask, forcing a composure I no longer feel.

Apparently, Chaplain Charlie feels the same way, minus my composure.

"Doctor, did you miss the med school class in patient sensitivity?"

Then as Frank and I watch in astonishment, Chaplain Charlie firmly takes the doctor's arm and escorts him out the door, saying, "I need some time alone with your patients. Thank you for coming."

Chaplain Charlie then turns on his heels, goes over to Frank's chair, and places his arm around Frank, who is visibly shaken.

"You do have some tough choices to make, but one thing's for sure, you do not have to take abuse from insensitive idiots who are supposed to be here to help. I think you should both have dinner together and talk about anything but medical stuff. On my next time here, I'll tell you about the crocodiles in my childhood schoolyard. You both need to think about something outside this hospital.

"Later, you can begin to make the tough decisions knowing there will be more choices than you imagine and better solutions to consider. And don't forget, I am here to help both of you through this. Frank, here is my pager number. If anyone even looks at you cross-eyed, you send for me."

I am learning that death is a nighttime business, and Chaplain Charlie is to be my guide on the journey. He has wisely sent Frank for a break by asking to please retrieve for him a much-needed cup of caffeine.

Chaplain Charlie sets up the chessboard on the portable table atop my bed, and then pulls out a paper bag containing the most ridiculous looking pointed, bright orange party hat and pops it on his head, pulling the rubber band under his chin. Then he puts on my head a candy-cane striped hat, pulling the elastic down over the oxygen tubing. Flinging his vivid stole over his shoulder, he rolls up his sleeves and barks loudly, "Grandfather! You make the first move."

I am in shock.

The chess game begins. One move and then another, we trade a few pawns. I warn this curious fellow about my skills.

"You know, my own father prepared me for being a good chess player."

"How's that, Gramps? You don't mind that I call you gramps, do you?"

"Gramps will do fine. Yeah, what I mean is growing up, my father would always tell me to keep my hand close to my heart. Don't show your feelings, on the chessboard, or off. Do not let on what your next move may be. And above all, never let them see you cry. Boys don't cry. Don't you know?"

"Your queen's in danger," Charlie responds. "You and your old man, were you close?"

"The last time we spoke was on the worst day of my life."

"Worst day? Sounds terrifying, mate." Chaplain flashes a smile as he takes the king's knight. "Check! Hey, after the past five games with you beating the crap out of me, it's about time you let me win."

I tell the chaplain, "That poor move, sir? Entirely my fault. I am a bit befuddled today. Anyway, according to my father, I operated under unnecessary emotions way too often. He considered me a failure. And the person I loved, my daughter, Faith? He told me I failed her too. It was after his statement that I walked out of the psychiatric hospital where Faith was in treatment and moved away. What kind of louse does that?"

"What is the truth, kind man? What does your instinct say?"

"I honestly don't know anymore. The quest for Faith has me set out on this cross-country trip with Frank. We came all the way from California in hope of finding her. There were many moments I thought this old ticker would not make it."

I move a pawn in his queen's knight's path and continue.

"My father told me Faith's illness was a problem to be solved, that Faith's behavior was due to my inability to change her condition. He said in front of several people, including my wife and daughter, 'You're a damned failure if you cannot captain your own ship.'"

Chaplain Charlie was ignoring the chessboard watching me closely.

"You see, I tried everything I could do for Faith and my wife. But, it didn't matter what I did. Faith became sicker and sicker. A man is supposed to solve and fix things. Years ago, as I stood in that psychiatric unit, I could only wring my hands in defeat. My wife cried in my arms, and I could not help her either."

I look across at Charlie with his pointed party hat, the comical stole, and unique getup that passes for his uniform. I break into unexpected, abandoned giggling. There is a tightness in my chest, but still, I continue laughing. Boy, did it feel good. Before I know it, Chaplain Charlie yells out, "*Yes*! Checkmate! I win, finally!"

Noticeably though like a serious, eternal turn, this wonderful sensation of laughter is turning to coughing, then I am gasping for air. My body is heaving now as I attempt to keep up with my emotions and growing chest pain.

"You are safe." I hear Charlie's voice, which seems to understand what I fear.

"I have come such a long way to find Faith. What if I don't? Why would she even want to see me? And if she won't, I have failed again."

"What is your intent, kind sir? What is your heart telling you?"

In between measured breaths, I am whispering, "To love her. I want to look into her eyes one more time and confess that I never stopped loving her. I understand so much more. Mental illness is no one's fault. I only want to find my Faith again. If only for a moment before—"

Chaplain Charlie pulls a guitar out of the closet and begins to strum the keys. Then a nurse appears suddenly out of nowhere, removes the pillows, and reclines the bed. The chaplain is now on one side of the bed, with the nurse on the other, and together they pull the blue blanket up under my chin. I feel so cold. The nurse places a pre-warmed coverlet atop the bedspread. I feel a needle enter the vein in my arm. Slowly, I feel as if I am sinking into a warm cocoon of safety. Chaplain Charlie smiles gently. In the stillness, I am only aware of beautiful music he has started playing.

Resting the guitar on his lap, Chaplain Charlie pauses.

"Grandpa, I hear many stories and have discovered many pearls among the swine. I once heard the story from a young man who was molested by his father. Well, I had read that sexual abuse changes that child's brain wiring. So for a long time, I could only see the tragedy. But I learned from that young man something you need to understand, too, about your daughter Faith. Her illness changed her brain to an extent, but it is not always a complete negative. Out of his pain and struggle, that boy became a compassionate soul, with a depth beyond his years. This profound aspect of change may very well have affected your Faith. Let's stop mourning what was lost and rejoice in what was created."

Chaplain Charlie must have thought that his new friend had drifted into a nap, but I opened my eyes to stare widely at him.

"I've been assuming only the worst and blaming myself all these years. It never occurred to me that leaving her life could give birth to something positive."

"Parents forget a vital fact in their children's lives, Grandpa. The child has her own higher power, and the parent is *not* it."

I snicker, which evolves into a cough again. "Are you trying to tell me that I'm not God, Chaplain? This is devastating news!"

Chaplain Charlie continues softly playing his guitar, while I drink some water, hoping the coughing will subside.

"Grandpa, if you don't mind me asking something? When people think about you, what is the last thing they would expect?"

I am no longer feeling the weight of the world upon my shoulders. Everything I worried about an entire life, insurmountable goals and life and death actions, is all fading into a mist. It seems now that what we call our personal reality is so much simpler than we make it. Why do we complicate time with so many layers of busy nonsense?

In this realization, a rare calm fills my body. I am becoming the freedom I have longed a lifetime for. My response flows out without thought or weight.

"I was down on myself, always. And you know what? I do believe in God, a spiritual being filled with love, minus judgment. God is not about condemnation but mercy and forgiveness. I learned this God working the twelve steps in AA. 'We came to believe that a power greater than ourselves could restore us to sanity.' The word 'restore' implies we were born sane in the first place."

I kept whispering, "I had a hard time letting go and trusting Faith would be in God's loving hands. I was so wrong. The worst part is I became cut off from the spirit of God by believing my own lies. All those years I hid behind my public personality, so afraid of inner secrets and knowledge of what I had done. But God saw through my vain cover-ups and loved me anyway. I admitted I was living a lie and talked to God about who I am. That was the day I began to plan this trip to find Faith.

"Chaplain, I believed my church shamed me as my own father had. Rules I could not understand, judgments and rejection by people who sat in Sunday pews, stares and gossip about the strange actions of my precious Faith. After a while, it all stopped making sense, and I left the church. I left religion. I guess I left God back in the church, didn't occur to me to take Him with."

"Please, Gramps, don't do that. 'Don't throw the baby out with the bathwater,' as my grandmother always said. God has nothing to do with men's actions. God has always been with you, is here with you now, and will always be.

"Judgment? Look at me? To some I look more like a cartoon character than a follower of God, yet inside, I carry the Lord's spirit, just like you, trying to live a good life. To answer my own question, when you look at my appearance, the last thing you would expect is that I am a minister of the faith. Now please, close your eyes and tell me, what is the last thing people would expect from inside you? That, my friend, is your essence."

I close my eyes and release. I feel the nurse layer another pre-warmed blanket, this one across my shoulders and chest. The calm increases. My chest pain is lessening now, and I feel this gentle stream of words come forward, "In my heart, I did know the truth. I stopped hiding what I did from God. All the years in California, I was so afraid of my past. But I found hope that I would hold Faith again. I sought the courage to seek God despite my frailty. I prayed. I had Frank call, and it went to voicemail. I told Faith I love her and asked forgiveness. I ask God for forgiveness too. Without God, my soul could never find rest on any other path.

"I must accept that Faith may never come to the hospital in time. I have done the footwork. I leave it in God's hands."

Chaplain Charlie continues softly playing a melody as I was speaking. His look is tender as he drums his guitar, singing to one of my favorite Metallica melodies, but with Charlie's distinct words. My eyes close.

"Relax, Gramps," he whispers, and his song fills the room with its repose.

God our eternal lover;
Original and everlasting love, Lord, Almighty
Heaven's peaceful realm.
On this, my final earthly day,
a soul yearns to return Home.
Suffering shadows, my spirit longs to find You.
The tempo slows as Chaplain Charlie whispers his chorus.
Where are you, Lord?
Body still, seeking release.
God, the eternal lover, waits in the valley of this time.
Call out; He comes running.
Wrap your arms around, I am alone and scared.
He slides besides You,
See our Lord's joyful tears. Now reach forward.
He is near. All is well.

The world is turning in slow motion as I sense her after all these years, sitting next to me in the hospital bed. She is radiant. How did mother get here?

"Mother?"

I am nine years old again, and she hears me from the living room sofa. I was hiding in my bedroom from my father's wrath should he find his son crying. Mother holds the hand of her child, looks sweetly, and says, "John, your father must not see you cry as he does not understand. He is not as you and I. We are born to live in this world but in a different way, and it is okay. People do not accept those who are different. But remember, *you* are my son. You march to the beat of a different drummer. You are beautiful. You are forgiven. And you are loved."

"Mother, mother. I have tried so hard to do the right thing in this life. But I have made so many mistakes. And then, Faith, she turned out to be as sensitive as I am. I tried so hard, Mother. I really did."

My eyes open when I no longer feel my mother's presence. There is a sea of frantic-looking people in white lab coats, blue scrubs, and Chaplain Charlie's brightly colored stole, falling to the floor.

All of a sudden, I feel a rush of cool air as the nurse brushes up against my cheek. She is reaching hastily for the button on the hospital intercom. I feel lightheaded, woozy with what can best be described as a global escape from tension and suffering.

"I have lived a good life," I murmur to myself, as the room's ceiling becomes a starry night sky.

From a distance, I hear the nurse's commanding voice. She is yelling, "Code Blue. Code Blue. Room 311. *Stat.*" She bangs on the metal button on the intercom system and barks even louder into the wall.

"Dr. Jacobs. Room 311. *Stat.* Dr. Jacobs. Room 311. *Stat.*"

"Respiratory therapy room 311. *Stat.*"

She sounds upset, and I wish I could tell her not to worry and that everything really is so simple. Nothing to fear when God is near. All really will be well.

But I can no longer speak.

Chapter 31

We are voyagers traveling day by day toward eternity. We do not find peace until we know our destination.

—Debra Marie DeLash

Hope
Hospital Family Waiting Room

Chaplain Charlie finishes his prayer outside grandfather's room and takes off in search of Frank. He finds Frank down the hall on the third-floor waiting room, tucked into the corner. He is surrounded by two empty bags of corn chips, five empty snicker bar wrappers, and four empty soda cans. Exhausted, Frank reclines on the sofa and stares dazed into space.

"Someone looks as if he had a hypoglycemic attack. Hope the sugar crash is easy on you. Hey, Frank, let's have a chat." Chaplain Charlie offers his famous grin.

A woman, who quietly stands to look out the window, turns around. She is conservatively dressed in wool pants and a blue cashmere sweater set. Though she has been traveling for hours, there are few wrinkles in evidence. Even her penny loafers are polished to a mirror finish. A carefully studied look of detailed perfection, this is not a woman who has fast-food containers on the floor of her car. Wearing a waist-length braid reminiscent of the 1960 hippie era, she can't be over forty years old. She looks over as if the chaplain is an uninvited nightmare.

"Who might you be, sir, if I may ask? And how do you know my son?"

"I am the hospital chaplain. Charlie's my name. Frank and I met when his grandfather was admitted to the hospital."

"That would be my father, John. John Goodwill."

Chaplain Charlie looks a bit confused and asks, "Oh, then you must be Faith. Your father has been waiting to see you."

"*No*! I am certainly not Faith! I am Hope, John's second daughter. I am sure he has spoken about me. He must have known I would be on my way."

"I apologize for my blunder, Hope. It's been a very long day. Okay, folks, let's sit down and have a chitchat. What do you say?"

"Sure, why not? Maybe you can give us information no one else seems to have." Hope relaxes a bit and leans toward Chaplain Charlie, obviously hungry for an update.

The three of them sit kitty-corner on the blue plastic sofas placed strategically within the room. Chaplain Charlie begins to speak.

"Over the past couple days, I have grown quite fond of your father, and grandfather, despite the fact that he manages to beat me at chess."

He smiles and continues, "He is not in any distress or panic. He seems remarkably at peace with whatever is happening with him. An hour or so ago, I was playing Metallica on the guitar, and he even said he liked it. We were wearing pointed party hats during the chess game. I think it helps me win, but I could be wrong. I often am."

Frank chuckles and relaxes his shoulders down from his ears, but Hope begins to wring her hands.

"Pointed hats, psychedelic silk stoles, and excuse me, sir, but why in God's name are you wearing a dyed orange daisy on your lapel? Is this a hospital or a circus?"

"Mom, do you have to be so rude? I know you are stressed. I am too, but Chaplain is the person holding this whole intensive care unit together. At least that is what I have observed. The nurses think so too, I'll bet."

"All right, all right. Chaplain? I apologize. I am at the end of my emotional rope. I haven't slept well since my father left on this cross-country trip with Frank. They have been chased by tornados and in and out of emergency rooms. I have flown out here once already, just to be sent home by my stubborn father."

She stops her rapid-fire speech and takes a deep breath, then continues, "What I need to know is not about music and games between the two of you, but how he is doing health-wise, among other practical things."

"Hope?"

"Yes."

"I came down here directly from your father's room. Dr. Jacob, our hospitalist, is with him right now. As a chaplain, I cannot speak about your loved one's medical condition. I am more interested in his soul and spiritual health."

"Well then, Chaplain?" Frank clears his throat and continues, "What kind of mood is Grandpa in?"

The chaplain does not hesitate to look Hope and Frank directly in the eyes. This is a moment he has spent with many anxious family members, and each one is a different challenge. He folds his hands in a silent prayer for guidance and patience.

"I have counseled many patients and their families, and I believe you need to prepare for Grandpa's departure before too long."

Hope begins to cry, stands up, and resumes her position looking out the window.

Charlie continues, "I can't tell you what happens when they leave. But I believe they go somewhere else when they are ready, and that it is a place where their individual spirit fits in with others who have also gone home. It is the journey they were born to make, eventually. This is one time as we leave this life when we are and must be, single-minded, and completely absorbed in our solitary path. We each and alone will meet our Creator. We will face God."

Frank has tears running down his cheeks, but he nods, understanding.

Chaplain's beeper goes off, and he looks at it and hands Frank a business card bearing his pager number. He promises to return to the waiting room as soon as possible. He reaches out and squeezes Frank's hand.

"I will not leave you folks alone until you ask me to." And with that last thought, he goes out the door and runs silently down the hall.

Chapter 32

Love is timeless, permanent, clear, truthful, and humble.

—Debra Marie DeLash

Hope and Frank
Hospital Family Waiting Room

Within a few minutes of Chaplain Charlie's exit, a tired-looking Dr. Jacobs walks into the waiting room. He carries a set of X-rays.

"What is happening with Grandpa? He seemed okay when I left for the cafeteria." Frank is frantically grasping at straws as he looks for reassuring signs in the doctor's expression.

Hope turns from the window and walks purposefully toward the doctor.

"How is my dad?" She pleads.

"From what I understand, Mr. Goodwill was resting in bed and listening to the Chaplain's guitar. The nurse said he had left a pleasant message for someone on the phone earlier. He had hung up smiling. Around an hour ago, Chaplain rang the button for the nurse. When she entered the room, your dad was already losing consciousness."

Dr. Jacobs went on to explain that Grandpa had undergone a massive stroke. He then held up the X-rays and explained the present condition of his lungs.

Frank studies the X-rays for a moment and shudders. "I am no doctor, but looking at those X-rays, I am frightened for Grandpa."

There were two large white spaces where normally there would be black. The doctor explains how both lungs are filled with fluid, which harbors the dreadful bacteria.

"There is very poor air exchange. The only way to keep your grandfather alive is to put him immediately on life support."

Franks quickly jumps in. "No! This would be Grandpa's worst nightmare. He does not want to be kept alive by machines. We've talked about this." He glances at his mother, hoping she will understand.

Hope, however, is shaking her head. She's not ready to make the giant leap this is leading to.

Dr. Jacobs continues, focusing on Hope with tired eyes. "It is not likely your dad will resume consciousness anytime soon. If and when he does, it is obvious his lungs are in terrible shape. They are not able to provide his body organs with enough oxygen. And the oxygen from the ventilator may aggravate his damaged lungs."

"Failing lungs sounds like a terrible way to die. He wouldn't want that." Frank watches his mother, waiting for her protest.

"But my dad, I mean, well, shouldn't we try something more? If we put him on the breathing tube, then he would have time to recover, right? Isn't there always a chance, doctor?" Hope clutches the doctor's sleeve, trying to pull the right answer out of him.

"Mom! Grandpa talked about this very scenario. We already know his wishes."

Frank pulls out a crumpled envelope from his jacket pocket which holds grandfather's last wishes. Hope grabs it from her son's trembling hands. She reads it and sighs so loud that for a moment Frank forgets to breathe. When on the road, grandfather had crossed out Hope's name and wrote in Frank's on the power of attorney.

The doctor scans the document Frank is handing him and nods at Frank and Hope.

"I agree with your father's wishes. Even if he did eventually have a partial recovery, it is likely he would live out his remaining days in a nursing home tied to oxygen tubes. People who have the foresight to make a living will are considering their future quality of life. They are arranging to die with dignity. He could die gasping for air or of heart failure as his heart attempts to pump enough oxygen to keep him alive. It is an awful way to go out, and his last moments could be spent in fear."

Hope and her son turn to hug silently, breathing together, finding acceptance together. Hope gently pulls away, pressing her right hand to Frank's cheek, tears streaming down both their faces. The decision has been made. They both turn to Dr. Jacobs and nod silently.

The doctor jumps into action. "Okay. I must go, as they might be putting him on life support right now. I will keep him comfortable and give IV medicine to keep his kidneys functioning. The kidneys will continue to filter out the toxins, so he may rest. For now, he is comfortable and feeling no pain. Please, excuse me."

And with that, Dr. Jacobs retrieves the X-rays and dashes down the hall to Grandpa's room. Please, God, let him make it in time to spare any more misery.

Chapter 33

I believe that confession and true repentance is a receiving of God's life back in your heart. A confessed soul goes forward with the boldness of spirit, a quickened step. You have reignited the light of salvation.

—Debra Marie DeLash

Hope and Frank
John Goodwill's Hospital Room

Hope carefully opens the door to her dad's room, as if she might wake him with the slightest sound. Frank follows closely behind. They move to his bed, each standing on opposite sides, reaching to hold his hands. Dad appears to be peacefully sleeping, in stark contrast to other intensive care rooms they pass by.

In dad's room, there are no annoying beeping machines and only one IV pole with medicine running down the tube into the back of his left hand. Most importantly, dad did not have the noisy machine swishing air into his lungs. They move two chairs closer to the bed, where they can sit down to wait. You could hear a pin drop.

"Dad, dad? Can you hear me?" Hope grabs her dad's hand; he feels so warm, but there is no response, no blinking of eyes, no squeezing hers. There is no indication that he is aware of their presence.

"I am relieved he is not suffering. Aren't you, Mom?"

"Yes, I am, but this is all happening so fast. And did you hear what that Chaplain said? He thought I was Faith. I can only hope

Faith is not on her way. It is all too much for dad to deal with. It's too much for *me* to deal with."

"Not now, Mom! This is not about you. Please try and remember this. There is a reason why Grandpa gave me power of attorney. Do you even know the enormity of the decision I just made on his behalf?"

"Of course I do. Which is why I am trying to ward off any further complications, uh for dad's sake, of course."

Frank cradles his face in his hands and sighs with exasperation. He recalls his grandfather teaching him the Serenity Prayer and reminds himself that his mother falls into the category of things he can't control.

"Knowing this is what Grandpa wants doesn't protect us from what we are about to witness."

"Yes, son, this may be the hardest thing you will ever experience," Hope's face softens a bit as she looks at him.

"No matter what comes about, I will stay here. I will stay by his side until Grandpa no longer needs me."

Hope grunts and begins to search the room vigorously. "Her phone number has to be in here somewhere. Damn it, where would he hide it?"

Faith's phone number is now Hope's obsession.

Frank glances over at the clock on the wall, which now ticks larger than life. It is 2:00 a.m. He watches nervously, hoping his mother cannot find the phone number that will throw things into chaos. There is no reasoning with her. She is trying to bring order and control back, whatever the cost.

Frank continues to watch the clock, mesmerized with the sweeping second hand making its rounds, feeling impatience at the creeping slowness of time. He makes a sobering discovery after an hour of alternating between the clock, the heart monitor, grandfather, and back to the clock. Grandpa's heart rate has dropped by ten beats per minute during the past hour. This process is both predictable and consistent. At this rate, Frank calculates, Grandpa's heart will stop beating around ten this morning.

He cringes, realizing he is speculating on when his grandfather will end his long life. Frank has never before pondered the sequence of how anyone naturally dies. But here he is actually witnessing it with only his thoughts for company. The hours inch by. Occasionally, he tells himself, "I'm too young for this."

Hope and Frank keep this strange vigil throughout the night, both wanting the ordeal to end but not to end. Hope has given up searching the room and, without the distraction, gives in to tears and tries to talk to her father. There is unfinished business, things that never got said, with the opportunity now lost forever. The list of things neglected seems to grow longer for her with each hour, and she is desperate to find a solution. Frank is saying the Serenity Prayer countless times to prevent bursting.

Hope gently puts her father's hand back down on the blanket and paces around the room. Periodically, she checks out the moon's slow progress across the sky from the window and then returns to his bedside. She calls out his name, hoping for a response each time. But it is useless.

The nurses come in to bring them coffee and monitor his vital signs occasionally, silently noting his chart, and leave. There is very little for them to do in this room.

They wait and wait. Around 7:00 a.m., Dr. Jacobs pokes his head in the door to say he is on his way to church and will be back by nine.

Frank glances at the heart monitor, and Grandpa's heart rate is down to fifty-five beats per minute. This is so very scary.

The long night is ending, and daylight finally breaks around eight. Grandpa's heart rate is just under thirty beats per minute. Frank wonders if his grandfather has any awareness at all of what is happening, or is he dreaming? What kind of dreams do the dying have?

Hope begins to panic as she sees the monitor and realizes what is happening.

"Dad, dad! You can't leave! Please, don't leave me all alone!"

A nurse enters and walks over to check her patient's blood pressure and pulse, though it all shows on the screens over his bed. She knows that time is slipping away and seems reluctant to leave the room.

Chapter 34

Our lives. If you could go back and choose one moment in time, a chance to do something differently, would you? When the storm is calmed, what is left in your clear reflection upon the still waters?
—Debra Marie DeLash

Faith Finds Her Father
Grandfather's Hospital Room

As Hope and Frank keep vigil at grandfather's bed, elsewhere, on the first floor of the hospital, a woman rushes past the pink lady volunteer at the welcome desk. There is no time for niceties or formalities.

Faith hits the elevator button to the third floor, knowing her father is dying in intensive care. Maybe he already has for all she knows. What she does sense is every minute counts and that all she has is the now. This moment in time is for the living and for the dying.

"*Drat!*" Faith pushes the button over and over. Out loud she yells, "I will have to run up the stairs. Darn hospitals!"

She grabs onto the stair railing, pulls up with one hand her long, denim jean skirt, and begins to climb. She struggles both with her right hip which was replaced last spring and arthritis throughout her back. Yet she is not aware of the pain as much as the seconds ticking as she races out of the stairwell and over to the third-floor nurse's station.

"Mr. Goodwill? Where is he, please?" The nurse at the desk stands up and walks around the counter to stand beside Faith.

"May I ask you, ma'am, who you are?"

"Who I am? I am Mr. Goodwill's daughter. I am his daughter."

As if out of nowhere, Chaplain Charlie appears to take Faith's hand. He slips an envelope gently into her palm.

"Nurse Amy, this is Faith. Mr. Goodwill is waiting for her arrival. And now that she is here, I believe we need to escort her to Mr. Goodwill's room, pronto!"

"Nice stole, Chaplain. Never seen so many vibrant colors in one piece of clothing. But you wear it well."

"Part of my character I suppose."

Chaplain Charlie places his arm around Faith and squeezes her in a gesture of reassurance.

"I believe, beloved one, you need to read this letter before we enter your father's room. There is not much time. Please, open it now."

Faith hurriedly tears open the letter. An audible gasp is heard as her eyes hit the yellow-lined paper. She starts to cry as she immediately recognizes the familiar scrawl of her father's. It is the same scrawl she read so many years ago in her daily lunch box notes.

"Chaplain, no time to read this. Let's just go!" She tucks it away without further pause.

"It's time then. Let's hurry!" And with that, Chaplain takes Faith's hand, and they begin to run.

Hope and Frank hear a loud noise in the hallway. The sound of boot heels grows louder and louder as Chaplain Charlie bursts through the door followed by the wearer of dark blue, high-heeled leather boots.

Frank looks up at the first interruption of silence in hours. He instantly notices the woman's long French braid, which is the exact twin to his own mom's braid, length and all. There is perhaps a bit more gray in the visitor's hair, which frames a face tanned and filled with anxiety.

A huge smile spreads across Frank's exhausted face, the only one for days. He stands up to greet his aunt Faith, then glances over at Grandpa. He says in a loud voice, "Finally, you must be Faith!"

Chapter 35

We fear what we do not acknowledge. Until it grows
in its own poison and you finally admit the flaws,
mistakes, weaknesses, vulnerabilities, being human.
No longer alone with God by our side.
                                    —Debra Marie DeLash

The Journey Home of John Goodwill

The relentless ticking clock announces that 9:00 a.m. is approaching. Everyone in the room is transfixed with watching the secondhand jump around the clock's face. It is a Sunday morning, and father's family is here. Chaplain Charlie and Faith stand at the foot of the bed, with Frank and Hope seated on each side of father's head.

The room has been silent except for monitoring equipment; no one has spoken for the hour since Faith entered the room. The air is so heavy with the spinning emotion emanating from each of those waiting. There has been little movement as if a spell might be broken if each made their presence known.

Father has not responded to anything and seems to rest comfortably in the coma, with no sign of physical discomfort. Frank and Hope know that, according to the reading on the heart rate machine, father has a little over an hour to live on this earth. Hope looks down at his right hand, continuing to wish he will return her squeeze with his fingers.

Frank, holding his grandfather's left hand, recalls what the old man had said about our passing from life. "Those terrible prolonged deaths, kept alive by machines? Demanded by family members who are acting out of guilt, fear, and their own unresolved issues? I do not want to go out that way, Frank. And no one can persuade me to. Each of us, when it comes time to die, has a partnership with his Creator about how he will breathe his last. The rest of the people have no vote in this process."

Frank can feel the tension radiating across the bed from his mother. She is attempting to control this situation as surely as she clings to her father's hand. Always been a control freak, Frank thinks, but this time she is going up against grandfather's strong will; he has already planned the whole thing out. He sees how frequently Hope's eyes flick to the foot of the bed, where her new half-sister stands, uninvited and unwanted by anyone, according to Hope. Frank sends up a small prayer that God keeps his mother under divine control.

This last mile of John Goodwill's journey is about making peace with who he is, which he could not do until he sees his first child, Faith. Does he continue to try and reach her in his mind when in a coma? Some who have been in comas come out of them saying that they remember many things. His heart and respiration are slowing, gracefully. Is grandfather aware we are here, or is he approaching the crowning pinnacle of his life toward which he has traveled since birth?

Hope stirs restlessly as she begins to call him back aloud. There is too much unfinished business with her father, so much more to understand. If she could only have even a half hour, ten minutes with him, alone, without all these others.

Frank begins to shift in his chair, feeling that his mother is about to blow. Hope looks at Faith and tries to calm the building steam she feels toward her long-lost sister. But her best intentions fly out the window as Hope cannot hold back another minute.

"We need to clear this room! Dad! He is weak, and I don't know how much more he can handle. This reunion and all is just too stressful. Look at him, for God's sake!"

All eyes turn to father. What is he thinking? Frank wonders if his mother really expects her father to sit up and agree with her. His grandfather is not responding.

"Dad, Dad! I need you. Please don't leave yet."

Chaplain Charlie has moved silently next to Hope and takes her hand.

"Come, my dear, walk with me for a few moments. The hospital has a beautiful chapel, and it is time for you to see it."

"*What*? Now? You fool. How can I leave? So many unanswered questions. They will die with my father, don't you see?"

"I believe your father cannot move on with you here. He already knows you feel his love. Go ahead. Give him a hug."

Hope searches for any remaining strength and leans tenderly over the bed. She embraces her father. Gripping her arms around his chest, she holds on devotedly, tears pouring down to spot her father's hospital gown.

"I need to memorize the way he feels. I don't ever want to forget. No. No. This does not feel right at all!"

Chaplain gently but with determination hurries Hope out of the room. They disappear into the hallway and are gone.

The door swings open. Dr. Jacobs has returned early from church, still grasping his Bible. He is out of breath. He glances over at his patient's heart rate and says, "Mr. Goodwill?" He looks up at the clock then over to Frank. "What a peaceful way to go," he says quietly. "This is the death I would wish for anyone who I love."

Frank bolts out of the room. Clearly shaken and overwhelmed, he leaves Faith shivering, her arms wrapped around her body which has lost its natural warmth. Conflicting emotions have been battling in her heart for hours, discomfort at Hope's obvious resentment, confusion at the sight of her dying father after so many decades, and gratitude for Frank's kindness.

Dr. Jacobs pulls one of the white cotton blankets from a nearby shelf and wraps it around Faith's shoulders.

"Go ahead. Move closer. He can still hear you."

"Yes, thank you." Faith hesitates then pulls an envelope from her backpack and walks toward the head of the bed.

Dr. Jacobs whispers, "I need to go retrieve his chart. I will return shortly."

Dr. Jacobs glances back at the duo and sees Faith reach to hold her father's hand. She is moving her mouth closer toward his head and appears intent to tell her father one last message. Finally allowing for privacy, Dr. Jacobs shuts the door behind him.

Faith hopes with all her heart that her father can hear what she is saying, as she speaks in his ear. She has read that people in a coma can hear and understand, and she is desperate to get through to him before he leaves.

"Father, you didn't cause anything that happened to me when I was sick. There was nothing you could have done to change my course. Some of it was to do with the sensitivities your grandmother had, which were passed on down to me. I still hear the voice we talked about, Father. And I am strong, and I survive. It helps me to help other people. Really. Please be at peace and believe that everything turned out just fine. Go to God knowing that I love you, and I always will."

*****

It is 10:30 a.m., and the hospital chapel is deserted except for Chaplain Charlie and Hope. There are four exquisite stained glass windows, which remain shut on this rainy Sunday morning. Even as they talk, you can hear the unsettled winds outside. An overgrown tree snaps every few minutes against one of the windows, just often enough to keep a person on edge.

"But I was such a good daughter. I don't understand any of this. Why did he bring Faith here? A month ago, I didn't even know she existed."

Chaplain Charlie calmly answers, "Dear one, as human beings, we live with three realities: We all have pain. We all need to have our pain acknowledged in mercy and truth. Our Higher Power God is our path to healing.

"You have had a shock that has you spinning even beyond your father's passing. Your father finally told you about a family secret. Secrets are not a healthy thing. You might be wondering what else he has kept from you. Try to understand that the only reason he never told you was the depth of his own shame.

"My precious child, your father knows you to be a good daughter. I can't tell you why he brought your sister here, outside of the fact that this needs to happen. What I know of your father is he is meant to leave this place, at this time. I don't know why life unfolds as it does. What I can tell you is that this reunion was not meant to hurt you in any way. As my wise mother used to say to bring me back down to earth, 'Charlie, everything is *not* about you.'"

"How could it not hurt me? I am the one who cares for father, and then she sweeps in at the last moment to take the spotlight. This is just plain selfish."

"Selfish on whose part, dear? Your father? Does he not have the right to do what he needs to as he dies? Selfish on Faith's part? She didn't ask for this. She didn't design it. She was summoned by your father. Do you really think he loves you less because he loves her too?"

Hope stares at one of the windows, watching the raindrops running down the colored glass.

"Dear, please, will you kneel down to pray with me? Come on, right here. Let us bow our heads."

"I am not much of a—" she protests.

Chaplain interrupts Hope, "Would you mind taking my arm? My knees are not what they used to be. Thank you so much. Now, would you hand me my guitar?"

Reluctantly, Hope passes him the guitar and kneels beside her peculiar companion.

Chaplain leans his hips back to rest on the cushioned bench as he begins to play the strings. The light pours through the stained glass window and lands onto his face.

For the first time, Hope notices his vulnerability. His face is wrinkled, and his upper eyelids droop, partially covering the corner of one eye. The skin on the top of his hands is thin, and you can see visible highways of veins traveling his arms. This man has seen the wear and tear of life. He was so energetic earlier that she didn't realize that he is older than he seems at first glance.

Chaplain nods at Hope, who starts to cry. She's shaking her head as if to rid her mind of the garbage of unwanted thoughts.

Chaplain explains softly, "Years ago, I discovered when I sing my prayers, they seem to come alive. Yesterday afternoon, I sat at your father's bedside and strummed a melody by the group Metallica. Younger folks to older folks have heard of this band and though not sung by church choirs, John enjoyed the original wordings I offered. Would you join me and sing along in his honor?"

He begins to sing softly, as Hope smiles politely.

> Whisper to my Lord,
> Hold me until it is light.
> I am now running towards the seashore;
> The waves so huge
> As they crash upon the sand.
> Taking my hand,
> I remind Him not to let go.

As chaplain sings in the chapel below, on the third floor in Father's room, Faith has crawled up onto his bed and molds her body into his. There remain mere inches between their heads upon the pillow. She tries to match his breathing, her hand on his ribs, feeling the slowing of his breath.

Dr. Jacobs has calmly reentered, releases the bed's guardrail, and stands watch over father, whose heart rate has slowed to fifteen beats per minute. Looking at the two of them on the bed, he could hardly tell where one body leaves off, and the other begins.

A tear from father's eyes travels and slides down between their cheeks.

Meanwhile, in the chapel, chaplain keeps singing his song,

> Behold I am with you,
> Keeping you wherever you go,
> And will bring you back to this land.

Hope calls out in anguish, "My mind won't rest. I know my father's time is ending. I may never see him *again*."

Chaplain's voice slides into a child's bedtime prayer, singing the last words grandfather said before he lost consciousness.

> And never leaving my side,
> we journey together
> out into the sea
> where the storm is passing

*****

Back on the third floor, final words flow through father's brain which is ending its journey:

> I open my eyes and I see the light,
> into the horizon and beyond.

Father's room emanates a peace beyond all understanding, a calm we will know only when at last we are on our own journey.

The heart machine has flatlined with grace, and Dr. Jacobs pushes the off button. He shines a small flashlight into Father's eyes, gently closes them both, and smoothly slides out the one IV line in his hand.

"I will leave you two alone," Dr. Jacobs says.

*****

His song finished, Chaplain Charlie gently places his guitar on the chapel bench. He looks to the center peak of the redwood fanned ceiling and thrusts both arms straight up overhead, loudly reciting the following prayer:

"We pray for our friend, father, and grandfather John Goodwill. We ask that his soul find mercy and eternal peace, as he takes his love of God and our love for him on his way. *Amen!*"

Hope stares at the rain-washed windows, the tears slowing on her cheeks. Her lips silently form the word, "Amen."

*****

"Rest well, Father." Faith places a kiss on her father's cheek. She picks up the envelope she had brought to his bedside and carefully returns it to her pocket. Putting her backpack on one shoulder, she leaves the ICU in search of her new nephew, Frank.

Faith and Frank sit together in the now empty room of John Goodwill where they talked, shared, and cried. Then Faith took leave and returned to her life in Maine. However, she realized from the first moment she set eyes on Frank, she had a message for him and somehow had to convince her new nephew to believe her.

Chapter 36

So faith, hope, love remain, these three; but the greatest of these is love.
—1 Corinthians 13:13, NAB

A Father's Farewell

My Beloved Faith,

Frank, your nephew, and I drove your half-sister Hope's RV, cross-county to find you, and if reading this letter, I did not make it in time. We traveled day and night, and though my words are late, please listen to what I say. I have spent a lifetime reliving the day I drove to California, leaving you and your mother behind. You deserve the truth about why I ran and my understanding of why I never returned.

My most cherished moment was when a little piece of heaven, our Faith, was born. Back in the 1950s, fathers were not allowed in hospital delivery rooms. I was directed to wait at the end of a long corridor, downing cold, black coffee. I could hear my Sarah screaming, and she sounded so scared. My emotions took over. I dashed down the hall, around the corner, ignoring the firm imperatives of medical folks, and burst through the doorway. As I focused my eyes on the bright overhead light, the doctor grabbed your squirming body, held you up in the air, and yelled, "It's a girl!" Every other moment pales in comparison to that precious snapshot in time.

I do not understand what happened in your brain chemistry that caused such turmoil in your teenage years. Your pain became mine, and I tried to run away from it, not realizing the choice I made, thinking temporary would become permanent. I could never find rest on any other path but the one back home to my Faith.

On this journey, I opened myself up to a curious band of characters who shared their own pain. Like you and me, all of us, really, these honest souls live with a cross to bear. I learned something so incredible I want to share with you.

If looking for answers to things of this world, you seek out the strong and proud, hoping for solutions. But if you need the truth, which stems from God's Kingdom, you will find it amongst the meek and lowly. I know now that to love is to be present for each other, though we are imperfect, frail, yearning, crying; we need to live true to who we are born to become.

You see, back in that dismal time when your mental illness raged, I listened to the wrong voices, ones not of faith nor hope. My own father would say, "You are a failure," because I could not solve my child's suffering. I listened to his words instead of my own inner voice, and the negative messages became a self-fulfilling prophecy. I see now that you did not need me to fix what was beyond my ability but that you needed your father to be there for you and to trust God with the rest.

I did not come back to you because I could not face what I had done. The guilt, fear, and shame placed an abyss between me on the West Coast and you on the East Coast. I believed I did not deserve a second chance. As my health was failing, I confessed my sins, which, left unrepented, continued to break my heart; and then I followed my soul's true calling, which was to find you again. And the people Frank and I met along the way, my time with Chaplain Charlie, helped tear down the veil of denial and shame, which clouded my spiritual eyes for so long.

I reunited with God and found mercy and forgiveness in these last days. I pray that you can forgive this old geezer and that you live your time on earth with freedom, joy, and purpose. Know in your spirit, dear one, though this may be hard for you to believe, despite my weakness, I never stopped loving you. No matter where I go, I will always love you. Faith, though perhaps unseen in your eyes, you have been my greatest blessing.

Love,
Father

When the just cry out, the LORD hears them, and from all their distress he rescues them.
—Psalms 34:18

About the Author

Debra's professional years are devoted to service. She has applied education in psychology and occupational therapy in many settings: acute care hospitals, long-term facilities, outpatient and inpatient rehab centers, acute psychiatric unit, mental health day treatment and suicide prevention programs, drug and alcohol treatment center, and brain injury community reintegration.

Eight years ago, Debra tapped into personal experiences to create hope for those she calls the "forgotten." She created a safe haven on the World Wide Web for those who live with mental illness or love someone with mental illness and addictions. There she shares realistic hope, resources, and community with those without support from others.

Debra has always loved the Lord and yet, like so many, struggles with spiritual battles. In June 2016, she started *Your Eternal Soul* to share raw, daily living temptations from her own life and give spiritual direction to people seeking mercy, forgiveness, and hope in the arms of a loving, just God. Touching many, *Your Eternal Soul* within two years is growing to help 43,000 and more people who are hurting and in pain.

Remembering at six years old, walking down a 1960s street and seeing a woman, homeless and angry, looking into her eyes, not understanding a child's smile, and exploding into a verbal tirade. Debra sensed there was another story behind this than her young mind could put into words. *Seeking My Daughter Faith: Parables from The Forgotten*, first in the *Your Eternal Soul* series, Debra brings together the message that has driven her entire life.

"If looking for answers to things of this world, you seek out the strong and proud, hoping for solutions. But when you search for truth which stems from God's kingdom, you will find it among the meek and lowly."

Married for thirty-one years, mother of four, grandmother of six, Debra lives in California with her family. She may be reached at youreternalsoulmay12@gmail.com.

CPSIA information can be obtained
at www.ICGtesting.com
Printed in the USA
BVHW072058210119
538283BV00007B/555/P